The Healthy **Air Fryer** Cookbook for Beginners

~ 2000+ ~

Days of Healthy, Tasty and Easy to Cook Recipes to Master the full Potential of Your Air Fryer.

Stella Hamilton

Table of Contents

Introduction

An Air Fryer is a magic revolutionized kitchen appliance that helps you fry with less or even no oil at all. This kind of product applies Rapid Air technology, which offers a new way how to fry with less oil. This new invention cooks food through the circulation of superheated air and generates 80% low-fat food. Although the food is fried with less oil, you don't need to worry as the food processed by the Air Fryer still has the same taste as the food that is cooked using the deep-frying method.

This technology uses a superheated element, which radiates heat close to the food, and an exhaust fan in its lid to circulate airflow. An Air Fryer ensures that the processed food is cooked completely. The exhaust fan located at the top of the cooking chamber helps the food to get the same heating temperature in every part in a short time, resulting in cooked food of the best and healthy quality. Besides, cooking with an Air Fryer is also good for those that are busy and do not have enough time. For example, an Air Fryer only needs half a spoonful of oil and takes 10 minutes to serve a medium bowl of crispy French fries.

In addition to serving healthier food, an Air Fryer also provides some other benefits to you. Since an Air Fryer helps you fry using less oil or without oil at all for some kind of food, it automatically reduces the fat and cholesterol content in food. Surely, no one will refuse to enjoy fried food without worrying about the greasy and fat content. Having fried food with no guilt is really a form of indulging your tongue. Besides having low fat and cholesterol, by consuming oil sparingly, you save some amount of money, which can be used for other needs. An Air Fryer also can reheat your food. Sometimes, when you have fried leftovers and reheat them, it will usually serve reheated greasy food with some addition of unhealthy reuse oil. Surely, the saturated fat in fried food gets worse because of this process. An Air Fryer helps you reheat your food without being afraid of extra oils that the food may absorb. Fried bananas, fish and chips, nuggets, or even fried chicken can be reheated so that they become as warm and crispy as they were before by using an Air Fryer.
Some people may think that spending some amount of money to buy a fryer is wasteful. I dare to say that they are wrong because actually, an Air Fryer is not only used to fry. It is a sophisticated multi-function appliance since it also helps you to roast chicken, make steak, grill fish, and even bake a cake. With a built-in air filter, an Air Fryer filters the air and saves your kitchen from smoke and grease.

An air Fryer is really a simple, innovative method of cooking. Grab it fast, and welcome to a clean and healthy kitchen.

01. <u>Crispy Ham Egg Cups</u>

Preparing time: 17 minutes
Number of portions: 2

Required Material:

- 4 eggs
- 4 slices deli ham
- 56 g shredded medium Cheddar cheese.
- 28 g diced green bell pepper.
- 2 tbsp. diced red bell pepper.
- 2 tbsp. diced white onion.
- 2 tbsp. full-fat sour cream.

Procedure step by step:

1. A piece of ham should be placed in the base of each of the muffin cups. In a big bowl, mix the eggs and sour cream together. Cut the vegetables into very small pieces with a sharp knife and add them to the pan. Toss well to combine.

2. Put the mixture of eggs into muffin tins that were already filled with ham. On top crumble Cheddar cheese.

3. Lay the cups ready in a pan and should insert them in an air fryer.

4. Adjust the temperature to 160° C, now cook for twelve mins. Are ready when they have a crust of golden-brown color.

1. Consume while is warm!.

Dietary composition:
Calories: 341; Protein: 25g; Fiber: 1g; Fat: 25g; Carbs: 4g

02. Olives and Kale

Preparing time: 25 minutes
Number of portions: 4

Required Material:

- 4 eggs; whisked
- 120 g kale; chopped.
- 75 g black olives, pitted and sliced
- 2 tbsp. cheddar; grated
- Cooking spray
- A pinch of salt and black pepper

Procedure step by step:

1. Eggs, and everything of the other ingredients (except the frying spray) should be mixed together in a mixing basin using a whisk.
2. Afterward, spray a pan with spray, and fill it with the mixture.
3. After you insert the pan in the fryer, leave inside the food (twenty mins - 182°C). Eat a warm breakfast!

Dietary composition:
Calories: 115; Fat: 9g; Fiber: 1g; Carbs: 3g; Protein: 7g

03. Stuffed Poblanos

Preparing time: 30 minutes
Number of portions: 4

Required Material:

- 227 g. spicy ground pork breakfast sausage
- 4 large poblano peppers
- 4 large eggs.
- 113 g full-fat sour cream.
- 113 g full-fat cream cheese; softened.
- 60 g canned diced tomatoes and green chiles, drained
- 8 tbsp. shredded pepper jack cheese

Procedure step by step:

1. Warm a medium saucepan. Crumble and brown ground sausage in the skillet until no pink remains. Drain the sausage fat. Break eggs into the pan, scramble, and heat until no longer runny.
2. Add cream cheese to sausage in a large bowl. Mix tomatoes and chopped chilies. Add eggs gently.
3. Cut the top of each poblano (four- to five-inch incision) in and eliminate the seeds and white part with a little knife. Make four filling parts and carefully place one in each pepper. Top each with pepper jack cheese.
4. Drop one pepper into the air fryer basket. Set a 15-minute timer and 175 degrees Celsius.
5. The peppers and cheese will be soft and toasted when cooked. Serve with sour cream.

Dietary composition:
Calories: 489; Protein: 28g; Fiber: 2g; Fat: 39g; Carbs: 7g

04. Raspberries Oatmeal

Preparing time: 20 minutes
Number of portions: 4

Required Material:

- 120 g coconut; shredded
- 60 g raspberries
- 480 ml almond milk
- ¼ tsp. nutmeg, ground
- 2 tsp. stevia
- ½ tsp. cinnamon powder
- Cooking spray

Procedure step by step:

1. Spraying the pan with cooking spray.
2. It is required to know the instructions provided by the manufacturer for using an air fryer, before cooking the dish.
3. Combine together the ingredients and cook at a temperature of 182°C for 15

minutes.

4. Make sure each guest has their own individual bowl.

Dietary composition:

Calories: 215; Fat: 14g; Fiber: 7g; Carbs: 20g; Protein: 4g

05. Bell Pepper Eggs

Preparing time: 25 minutes
Number of portions: 4

Required Material:

- 4 (580g) green bell peppers
- ¼ medium onion; peeled and chopped
- 85 g. cooked ham; chopped
- 8 large eggs
- 120 g mild Cheddar cheese

Procedure step by step:

1. Eliminate the tops from each individual bell pepper. Using a sharp knife, scrape off the seeds and the white membranes that surround them. Ham and onion should be stuffed into each pepper.
2. Scramble two eggs in each of the peppers. Sprinkle cheese on top of each pepper. Put the ingredients into the basket of the air fryer.
3. Bring the temperature up to 199 degrees Celsius, and then turn the timer forward by 15 minutes. When everything is done cooking, the peppers will be soft, but the eggs will be solid. Prepare and serve at once.

Dietary composition:

Calories: 249; Protein: 18g; Fiber: 2g; Fat: 17g; Carbs: 7g

06. Avocado Cauliflower Toast

Preparing time: 23 minutes
Number of portions: 2

Required Material:

- 1 (340 g.) steamer bag of cauliflower
- 60 g shredded mozzarella cheese
- 1 large egg
- 1 ripe medium avocado
- ½ tsp. garlic powder.
- ¼ tsp. ground black pepper

Procedure step by step:

1. Follow the package instructions for cooking the cauliflower. Lay flat on cheesecloth or a dry towel to soak up any leftover moisture after removing from the bag.
2. Combine the cauliflower, egg, and mozzarella in a large bowl. Line your air fryer with parchment paper before using it.
3. Divide the cauliflower mixture in half and place each half on a separate sheet of paper. The cauliflower should be diluted until it can be sliced into quarter-inch thick slices. Using parchment paper in an air fryer is a must.
4. Put it in the oven and set the timer for 8 minutes at 200 degrees Celsius. Halfway through cooking time, turn the cauliflower over.
5. After 5 minutes with the cauliflower and the parchment paper, take it out of the oven.
6. To enjoy an avocado, you must first remove the pit. Remove the pulp and combine it with smashed garlic and freshly ground black pepper in a medium bowl. Put it on the cauliflower for flavor.

Dietary composition:

Calories: 284; Protein: 15g; Fiber: 7g; Fat: 23g; Carbs: 10g

07. Blackberries Bowls

Preparing time: 20 minutes
Number of portions: 4

Required Material:
- 360 ml coconut milk
- 40 g coconut; shredded
- 70 g blackberries
- 2 tsp. stevia

Procedure step by step:
1. Place the shredded coconut and the milk, cranberries, and stevia in the pan suitable for your air fryer. Mix well and put in the oven.
2. For cooking, the temperature must be at 180°C, for a quarter of an hour.
3. Enjoy your breakfast!

Dietary composition:
Calories: 157; Fat: 14g; Fiber: 3g; Carbs: 9g; Protein: 2g

08. Air Fryer Breakfast Frittata

Preparing time: 15 minutes
Time needed to cook: 20 minutes
Number of portions: 2

Required Material:
- 113 g crumbled breakfast sausage
- 4 lightly beaten eggs, 60 g cheese type Monterey Jack, shredded
- (0.5 g) cayenne pepper, two tbsp sliced red bell pepper
- A single green onion, chopped

Procedure step by step:
1. Prepare a Teflon cake pan that measures 6x2 inches and preheat the air fryer to 365 degrees Fahrenheit.
2. Mix the eggs, sausage, green onions, bell pepper, cheese, and cayenne together in a large bowl using a whisk.
3. Then, when the egg mixture has been prepared, place the cake pan in the Air fryer.
4. Reheat it for around 20 minutes after it has finished cooking.

Dietary composition:
Calories: 384, Fat: 30g, Carbohydrates: 2g, Sugar: 1g, Protein: 24g, Sodium: 586mg

09. Breakfast Pockets

Preparing time: 15 minutes
Time needed to cook: 30 minutes
Number of portions: 4

Required Material:
- 2 sheets: 487.6g almond flour puff pastry, cut into 4 equal-sized pieces
- 1 package: 170g ground breakfast sausage, crumbled
- 2 eggs, lightly beaten
- 113 g shredded cheddar cheese
- A single tsp salt, Half tsp black pepper
- 2 TBSPs canola oil

Procedure step by step:
1. Preheat the air fryer to 190°C and oil the basket.
2. Roast the sausages in the basket for 15 minutes.
3. Put the eggs in the basket and set a five-minute timer.
4. After seasoning split egg sausage mixture between the four puff pastry rectangles and top with cheese.
5. Top with shredded cheddar cheese and spray canola oil.
6. Cook a egg pocket in the basket for six minutes at 204 degrees Celsius. Repeat with each pocket.
7. Take away pockets from your Air-Fryer. Serve hot, enjoy.

Dietary composition:
Calories: 699, Fats: 57g, Carbs: 26g, Sugar: 1g, Proteins: 25g, Sodium: 1267mg

10. Ham and Egg Toast Cups

Preparing time: 5 minutes
Time needed to cook: 5 minutes
Number of portions: 2

Required Material:

- 2 eggs
- 2 slices (60 g) of ham
- Salt
- 2tbsp butter
- Cheese-type cheddar, for topping
- Black pepper, to taste

Procedure step by step:

1. Start the air fryer to reach 204 degrees Celsius, meanwhile, brush each ramekin with melted butter to prepare for the recipe.
2. Place a piece of ham in each of the ramekins that have been buttered, and then break an egg on top of each slice of ham.
3. After seasoning the food with spices and cheese, insert the basket with the ramekins in an air fryer.
4. After about five minutes, remove the ramekins from the basket.
5. Served warm.

Dietary composition:

Calories: 241, Fat: 20g, Carbs: 1g, Sugar: 0g, Protein: 14g

11. Broccoli Cheese Quiche

Preparing time: 10 minutes
Time needed to cook: 40 minutes
Number of portions: 2

Required Material:

- 1 large broccoli, chopped into florets
- 3 large carrots, peeled and diced
- 113 g cheddar cheese, grated
- 28 g feta cheese
- 2 large eggs

- Two tsp thyme and rosemary (one of each)
- Spices (salt &pepper)

Procedure step by step:

1. Thermostat of air fryer to 182 degrees C, then prepare a pie dish with spray.
2. Broccoli and carrots go cooked in a food cooker for about 20 minutes.
3. Mix milk, salt, dried herbs, eggs, and black pepper together with a whisk.
4. Put steamed veggies in the bottom of the quiche pan and tomatoes and cheese on top.
5. Fill the pie tin with the egg mixture and insert it in the Air fryer.
6. Prepare for about 20 mins and serve immediately when ready.

Dietary composition:

Calories: 438, Fat: 32g, Cholesterol: 324mg, Sodium: 834mg, Carbohydrates: 15g, Fiber: 5g, Sugars: 6g, Protein: 24g

12. Brioche Sausage

Preparing time: 10 minutes,
Time needed to cook: 15 minutes;
Serve: 4

Required Material:

- 2 sausages
- 2 breadsticks

Direction:

1. Take away the bread crumb to create a hollow cylinder (make pieces of about 10 cm, otherwise they will be hard to work).
2. Put the sausage in one half of the bread and cut 2 cm slices.
3. Put six slices in the basket.
4. Cook for 10 minutes at 160°C, rotating the crispy rolls after 5/6 minutes. Serve hot.

Dietary composition:
Calories: 195, Fat: 9g, Cholesterol: 30mg, Sodium: 415mg, Carbohydrates: 19g, Fiber: 1g, Sugars: 1g, Protein: 9g

13. Egg Veggie Frittata

Preparing time: 10 minutes
Time needed to cook: 18 minutes
Number of portions: 2

Required Material:
- 4 eggs
- 120 ml milk
- 2 green onions, chopped
- 60 gr baby Bella mushrooms, chopped
- 20 gr spinach, chopped
- A mix tsp pepper and salt of sea
- Dash of hot sauce

Procedure step by step:
1. Butter a 6x3-inch square pan and preheat the air fryer to 185 degrees C.
2. Mix together eggs, milk, and chopped vegetables.
3. Add salt, black pepper, and hot sauce and pour into the pan.
4. Air-fry for 18 minutes. Enjoy!.

Dietary composition:
Calories: 195, Fat: 13g, Cholesterol: 391mg, Sodium: 632mg, Carbs: 4g, Fiber: 1g, Sugar: 2g, Protein: 15g

14. Corn Pudding

Preparing time: 1 hour 25 minutes
Number of portions: 6

Required Material:
- 4 bacon slices; cooked and chopped.
- 3 eggs
- 3 cups bread; cubed
- 120 ml heavy cream
- 355 ml whole milk

- 100 g cheddar cheese; grated
- 400 g corn
- 120 g sweet pepper
- A chopped yellow onion.
- 60 ml celery.
- 1 tsp. thyme.
- 2 tsp. garlic; grated
- 3 tbsp. cheese, type Parmesan
- A single tbsp EVO oil

Procedure step by step:
1. Warm oil in a pan. Stir in corn, celery, thyme, onion, sweet pepper, salt, spices, and garlic; sauté for 15 minutes, and pass on to a mixing bowl.
2. Add bacon, pepper, eggs, milk, cream, salt, bread, and cheddar cheese to the bowl. Stir and place into an air fryer-compatible casserole dish.
3. Fry at 180°C for 30 minutes.
4. Distribute parmesan cheese on pudding and cook for another 30 minutes. Cut and provide.

Dietary composition:
Calories: 436, Fat: 24g, Cholesterol: 161mg, Sodium: 587mg, Carbs: 34g, Sugar: 10g, Fiber: 3g, Protein: 21g

15. Delicious Doughnuts

Preparing time: 28 Minutes
Number of portions: 6

Required Material:
- 120 g sugar
- 270g white flour
- 1 tsp. cinnamon powder
- 2 egg yolks
- 80 g caster sugar
- 4 tbsp. butter; soft
- 1 ½ tsp. baking powder
- 120 ml sour cream

Procedure step by step:

1. Mix butter, sugar, egg, half part sour cream.
2. After a good mixing add flour and baking powder to mixture already prepare.
3. Amalgamate well to create a dough, then move it to a surface that is floured, roll it out, and cut large circles and smaller ones in the middle.
4. Apply the remaining part of the butter on the doughnuts and fry them at 180 degrees C for 8 minutes.
5. Combine cinnamon and caster sugar on a small plate. Serve doughnuts with cinnamon and sugar.

Dietary composition:
Calories: 427, Fat: 13g, Carbohydrates: 72g, Protein: 7g, Fiber: 1g, Sugar: 36g, Sodium: 166mg

16. Blackberries and Cornflakes

Preparing time: 15 minutes
Number of portions: 4
Required Material:

- 710 ml milk
- 60 g blackberries
- 2 eggs; whisked
- 1 tbsp. sugar
- 1/4 tsp. nutmeg; ground
- 4 tbsp. cream cheese; whipped
- 120 g cornflakes

Procedure step by step:

1. Place all of the ingredients in a container and give them a thorough toss.
2. Warm your fryer to 176 degrees Celsius, then add the cornflakes mixture, smooth it out, and put it in your air-fryer for ten mins. Distribute between dishes, and have fun.

Dietary composition:
Calories: 332, Fat: 12g, Sodium: 347mg, Cholesterol: 109mg, Fiber: 2g, Sugar: 22g, Carbs: 44g, Protein: 12g

17. Pancakes

Preparing time: 30 minutes
Number of portions: 4
Required Material:

- 400 g white flour
- 240 ml apple; peeled, cored and chopped.
- 300 ml milk
- 1 egg; whisked
- Sugar: 2 tbsp.
- 2 tsp. each, powdered baking and cinnamon
- A quarter tsp. extract of vanilla
- Cooking spray (for greasing)

Procedure step by step:

1. First, whisk together everything in an ample dish.
2. Spray a frying pan with cooking spray, and then add a quarter of the dough.
3. Wrap in foil and cook for 5 minutes at 182 °C, turning once.
4. Repeat phases 2 and 3 with the remaining dough three more times. Serve the pancakes straight away.

Dietary composition:
Calories: 438, Fat: 4.4g, Protein: 12g, Cholesterol: 52mg, Carbs: 87g, Sodium: 438mg, Fiber: 3.1g, Sugar: 20g,

18. Creamy Mushroom Pie

Preparing time: 20 minutes
Number of portions: 4
Required Material:

- 6 white mushrooms; chopped.
- 3 eggs
- 1 red onion; chopped.
- 9-inch pie dough
- 30 g cheddar cheese; grated
- 120 ml heavy cream
- 2 tbsp. bacon; cooked and crumbled
- A single tbsp. EVO oil
- Half tsp. thyme; dried

Procedure step by step:

1. Stretch the dough on a plane surface, then pass it on to an air fryer-compatible pie pan after greasing.
2. Stir every component except for the cheese in a dish and put it inside the pie pan.
3. Then, sprinkle with the cheese and bake at 200 degrees Celsius for a total of ten minutes. Slice and serve.

Dietary composition:
Calories: 444, Total Fat: 31g, Saturated Fat: 13g, Cholesterol: 224mg, Sodium: 464mg, Total Carbohydrate: 26g, Dietary Fiber: 1g, Total Sugars: 2g, Protein: 15g

19. Cheesy Hash Brown

Preparing time: 30 minutes
Number of portions: 6
Required Material:

- 600 g. hash browns
- 6 bacon slices; chopped.
- 227 g. cream cheese; softened
- 1 yellow onion; chopped.
- 6 eggs
- 6 spring onions; chopped.
- 240 ml cheddar cheese; shredded
- 240 ml almond milk
- A drizzle of EVO oil, Salt & Pepper

Procedure step by step:

1. The first step is to heat your air fryer to 175 degrees Celsius with the oil inside.
2. Combine together all of components, excluding the spring onion, and set aside.
3. Place the contents of this combination in the fryer, covering it, and letting it cook for 20mins.
4. Distribute the mixture evenly among the plates, top with the spring onions, and serve.

Dietary composition:
Calories: 502, Total Fat: 38g, Saturated Fat: 18g, Cholesterol: 278mg, Sodium: 581mg, Total Carbohydrate: 20g, Dietary Fiber: 2g, Total Sugars: 2g, Protein: 21g

20. Pear Oatmeal

Preparing time: 17 minutes
Number of portions: 4
Required Material:

- 240 ml milk
- 55 g brown sugar
- 60 g walnuts; chopped.
- 480 g pear; peeled and chopped.
- 120 g oats, old-fashioned
- Half tsp. cinnamon in powder
- A tbsp. butter; softened

Procedure step by step:

1. Put everything in an air fryer-safe dish and give it a good swirl before placing it in the air fryer. 15 minutes at 360 degrees Fahrenheit is the recommended frying time. Use separate bowls for each guest

Dietary composition:
Calories: 393, Fat: 14g, Sodium: 53mg, Cholesterol: 16mg, Carbs: 65g, Fiber Total: 8g, Sugar Total: 36g, Protein: 8g

21. Parmesan Zucchini Rounds

Preparing time: 25 minutes
Number of portions: 4

Required Material:

- 4 zucchinis; sliced
- 180 g parmesan; grated
- 15 g parsley; chopped.
- 1 egg; whisked
- 1 egg white; whisked
- ½ tsp. garlic powder
- Cooking spray

Procedure step by step:

1. Grab a bowl, add the whole egg and white egg, parmesan cheese, parsley, and powdered garlic, and whisk all of the ingredients together.
2. Dip each slice of zucchini in this mixture, then set them all in the tin of your air fryer, after spraying with spray (use cooking spray), and cook them at 185 degrees Celsius for 20mins.
3. Distribute evenly among the plates, and serve as the main course.

Dietary composition:
Calories: 201; Fat: 12,4g; Fiber: 1,6g; Carbs: 7,1g; Protein: 16,2g

22. Green Bean Casserole

Preparing time: 25 minutes
Number of portions: 4

Required Material:

- 454 g fresh green beans, edges trimmed

- 14 g pork rinds, finely ground
- 28 g full-fat cream cheese
- 118 g heavy whipping cream.
- 59 g diced gold onion
- 118 g white mushrooms
- 118 g chicken broth
- 4 tbsp. unsalted butter.
- ¼ tsp. xanthan gum

Procedure step by step:

1. In a medium-size pan soften the butter. About three to five minutes into the sautéing process, the onion and the mushrooms should have grown tender and aromatic.
2. Incorporate the heavy whipping cream, cream cheese, and chicken stock. Mix well with a whisk. When to start a boil reduce the heat for a few minutes. Remove the pan from the flame after sprinkling it with xanthan gum, and leave set it aside.
3. Chop the green beans and put them in a circular baking dish, about a capacity of 4 cups. After pouring the sauce mixture over them, toss them together and cover everything. Grounded pig rinds should be sprinkled on top. insert the ingredients into the basket of the air fryer.
4. Bring the temperature up to 160 degrees Celsius, and then turn the timer forward by 15 minutes. When everything is done, the top will be golden, and the green beans will be fork soft. Enjoy it hot.

Dietary composition:
Calories: 304; Protein: 5g; Fiber: 2g; Fat: 29g; Carbs: 7g

23. Zucchini Spaghetti

Preparing time: 20 minutes
Number of portions: 4

Required Material:

- 453.6 zucchinis, cut with a spiralizer
- 100 g parmesan; grated
- 15 g parsley; chopped.

- 60 ml olive oil
- 6 garlic cloves; minced
- half tsp red pepper flakes

Procedure step by step:

1. Combine all of the components in a pan that is compatible with your air fryer, and give it a toss.
2. Place it in the fryer, adjust temperature to 187 degrees Celsius. Cook for 15 minutes.
3. Distribute the mixture among the dishes, and serve it as an accompaniment to the main dish.

Dietary composition:
Calories: 326; Fat: 27g; Fiber: 2g; Carbs: 9g; Protein: 13g

24. Cabbage and Radishes Mix

Preparing time: 20 minutes
Number of portions: 4

Required Material:

- 1420 g green cabbage; shredded
- 120 g celery leaves; chopped.
- 60 g green onions; chopped.
- 6 radishes; sliced
- 3 tbsp. olive oil
- 2 tbsp. balsamic vinegar
- ½ tsp. hot paprika
- 1 tsp. lemon juice

Procedure step by step:

1. Start by cleaning and chopping the onion, cabbage, radish, and celery.
2. Take a large enough dish, put the vegetables in it, and incorporate the other components from the list. Mix well to blend the flavors.
3. Pour everything into a pan for the fryer and cook for a quarter of an hour at 193°C.
4. When ready, serve by dividing it into four plates. Enjoy this delight

Dietary composition:
Calories: 137; Fat: 10g; Fiber: 4g; Carbs: 11g;
Protein: 2g

25. Jicama Fries

Preparing time: 30 minutes
Number of portions: 4

Required Material:

- 1 small jicama; peeled.
- A quarter tsp each powder (pepper, onion, garlic)
- ¾ tsp. chili in powder

Procedure step by step:

1. Chop the jicama into pieces about the size of matchsticks.
2. Put the pieces in a small dish, then sprinkle them with the other ingredients. Put the fries in the basket of your air fryer.
3. Bring temperature up to 175°Celsius, and then turn the timer forward by 20 minutes. During the cooking process, you should rotate the basket two or three times. Enjoy warm.

Dietary composition:
Calories: 55; Protein: 1g; Fiber: 6g; Fat: 0.3g;
Carbs: 13g

26. Bacon Wrapped Onion Rings.

Preparing time: 15 minutes
Number of portions: 4

Required Material:

- 1 large onion; peeled.
- 8 slices sugar-free bacon.
- 1 tbsp. sriracha

Procedure step by step:

1. Cut the onion into slices that are a quarter of an inch thick. Sriracha should be brushed all over the onion pieces. If you take two rings of onion and wrap them with bacon, that makes four rings. It

should be repeated with the remaining bacon and onion.
2. Second, place the items in the cooking basket. Put it in the oven preferably at 175 degrees Celsius for just 10 mins.
3. Flip the onion rings over to ensure even cooking, only one time. Bacon should be crisp when it is ready.

Dietary composition:
Calories: 207; Protein: 14g; Fiber: 1g; Fat: 14g;
Carbs: 5g

27. Cheesy Meatballs

Preparing time: 30 minutes
Number of portions: 16 meatballs

Required Material:

- 454 g. 80/20 ground beef.
- 85 g. low-moisture, whole-milk mozzarella, cubed
- 1 large egg.
- 120 ml low-carb, no-sugar-added pasta sauce.
- 25-30 g grated Parmesan cheese.
- 25-30 g blanched finely ground almond flour.
- A quarter tsp. onion plus half of garlic
- 1 tsp. dried parsley.

Procedure step by step:

1. Beef, almond meal, parsley, garlic and onion powder, and a single egg should be mixed together. Mixing the components well by folding them together.
2. Roll the mixture into balls, and use your thumb or a spoon to make a hole in the middle of each meatball. Put a cheese cube in the middle, and then roll the dough around it to make a ball.
3. Insert the meatballs into the fryer for cooking, prepare in batches if required.
4. Make the necessary adjustments so that the temperature is 175 degrees Celsius, and then set the timer for 15 minutes.
5. When the outside will have a tiny crunch

to it, and the inside are 80°C the meatballs will be thoroughly cooked.

6. When the meatballs are done cooking, throw them in the sauce and top each dish with some grated Parmesan cheese.

Dietary composition:
Calories: 115; Protein: 8.8g; Fiber: 0.5g; Fat: 8.1g; Carbs: 1.7g

28. Jalapeño Bacon Cheese Bread

Preparing time: 25 minutes
Number of portions: 8 sticks

Required Material:

- 4 slices sugar-free bacon; cooked and chopped
- 2 large eggs.
- 60 g chopped pickled jalapeños.
- 23 g grated Parmesan cheese.
- 226g shredded mozzarella cheese

Procedure step by step:

1. Combine all ingredients. Cut paper bake for your fryer basket and put in.
2. Press the mixture into a circle using your hands. Depending on your fryer, you may need to make two smaller cheese breads.
3. Put cheese bread in the fryer.
4. The clock go for 15mins at a temperature of 160 degrees C. Rotate the bread at 5 minutes from the end. The surface is golden brown when baked. Serve hot.

Dietary composition:
Calories: 182; Protein: 14.7g; Fiber: 0.1g; Fat: 13.2g; Carbs: 1.8g

29. Peppers and Cheese Dip

Preparing time: 25 minutes
Number of portions: 6

Required Material:

- 2 bacon slices, cooked and crumbled
- 113 g. parmesan; grated

- 113 g. mozzarella; grated
- 227 ml. cream cheese, soft
- 2 red peppers
- Use to taste spices

Procedure step by step:

1. Combine everything in an air fryer-safe pan and give it a good whisking.
2. Cook the meal for 20 minutes at 200 degrees Celsius in a deep fryer. Refrigerate once in bowls.

Dietary composition:
Calories: 291; Fat: 26.5g; Fiber: 0.3g; Carbs: 3.7g; Protein: 11.8g

30. Avocado Bites

Preparing time: 13 minutes
Number of portions: 4

Required Material:

- 4 avocados, peeled, pitted, and cut in pieces
- 180 g almond meal
- Cooking spray
- 1 egg; whisked
- Pepper (Black) and a dash salt

Procedure step by step:

1. Place the almond meal and the egg in two separate bowls.
2. Sprinkle salt and pepper on the pieces of avocado, then dip them in egg, and then dredge them in almond meal.
3. Lay the avocado bites in the basket of your fryer, spray them with cooking spray, and set the temperature to 200 degrees Celsius. Cook for 8 minutes. Serve right away as a light snack.

Dietary composition:
Calories: 402; Fat: 34.8g; Fiber: 14.8g; Carbs: 20.1g; Protein: 11.3g

31. Easy Veggie Rolls

Preparing time: 30 minutes
Number of portions: 1
Required Material:

- 2 potatoes [mashed]
- 60 g peas
- 60 g carrots [mashed]
- 1 cabbage [small; sliced]
- 60 g beans
- 2 TBSPs sweet corn
- 1 onion [small; chopped]
- 1 tsp capsicum
- 1 tsp coriander
- 2 TBSP butter
- ginger garlic
- A half tsp masala in powder
- 50 g breadcrumbs
- Half tsp chili
- 1 packet roll sheets
- 120 ml cornstarch slurry

Procedure step by step:
1. Boil water after have put it in a pot and place all vegetables in a colander to drain and dry.
2. Stretch down the roll sheet and lay the filling on it; next, wrap up the filling and dip it in the slurry before rolling it in breadcrumbs.
3. Leave fry only 10 mins the food after your Air-Fryer reaches 189 degrees Celsius. Serve with rice that has been already boiled, and have a delectable meal.

Dietary composition:
Calories: 1200, Fat: 33g, Cholesterol: 64mg, Sodium: 1370mg, Carbohydrates: 208g, Fiber: 30g, Sugar: 30g, Protein: 39g

32. Special Grilled Cheese

Preparing time: 25 minutes
Number of portions: 2
Required Material:

- 4 slices of brioche or white bread
- 120 ml sharp cheddar cheese
- 60 g butter; melted

Procedure step by step:
1. Air Fryer to 180°C. Cheese and butter go put in different dishes. Butter each piece of bread.
2. Spread cheese on 2 of the 4 bread slices. Place the grilled cheese in the frying basket.
3. Fry to melt cheese and have golden brown (5–7 minutes).

Dietary composition:
Calories: 526, Fat: 42g, Saturated Fat: 25g, Cholesterol: 116mg, Sodium: 698mg, Carbohydrates: 24g, Fiber: 1g, Sugar: 3g, Protein: 16g

33. Different Potatoes Gratin

Preparing time: 55 minutes
Number of portions: 4
Required Material:

- 120 ml milk
- 7 medium russet potatoes; peeled
- 1 tsp black pepper
- 120 ml cream
- 60 g semi-mature cheese; grated
- 1/2 tsp nutmeg

Procedure step by step:
1. Warm the Air Fryer to 198°C. Shred potatoes, meanwhile.
2. Combine milk, cream, salt, pepper, and nutmeg in a bowl. Apply this to potato slices.
3. Place potato slices in a heat-resistant baking dish. Ladle the remaining liquid compost over the potatoes.
4. Turn on the Air Fryer for 25 mins and put the baking dish in the cooking basket.
5. Take out the cooking basket and spread the cheese over the potatoes. Gratin for 10 minutes.

Dietary composition:
Calories: 405, Fat: 20g, Sodium: 143mg, Sugar: 3g, Carbos: 44g, Cholesterol: 64mg, Protein: 11g,

Fiber: 4g

34. Hummus Mushroom Pizza

Preparing time: 20 minutes
Time needed to cook: 6 minutes
Number of portions: 4

Required Material:

- 4 Portobello mushroom caps, stemmed, and gills removed
- 85 g zucchini, shredded
- 2 TBSPs sweet red pepper, seeded and chopped
- 4 Kalamata olives, sliced
- 120 ml hummus
- 1 TBSP balsamic vinegar
- A dash Salt and (black) pepper
- 4 TBSPs pasta sauce
- One single garlic clove
- 1 tsp dried basil

Procedure step by step:

1. Pre-warm the air fryer to 165°C and oil the basket.
2. Brush vinegar on all Portobello mushrooms. Salt and pepper each mushroom cap.
3. Fill each mushroom with sauce and garlic.
4. Cook in the fryer for 3 minutes.
5. Unite zucchini, red peppers, and olives. Then sprinkle basil and spices.
6. Bake for another 3 mins and serve.
7. Serve mushroom pizzas with hummus accompaniment.

Dietary composition:
Calories: 146, Fat: 8g, Sodium: 366mg, Carbs: 15g, Fiber: 5g, Protein: 7g, Sugar: 5g

35. Rice Flour Crusted Tofu

Preparing time: 15 minutes
Time needed to cook: 28 minutes
Number of portions: 3

Required Material:

- 1 block (396 g) firm tofu, pressed and cubed into ½-inch size
- 2 TBSPs cornstarch
- 30 g rice flour
- A dash Salt
- Two tbsp Oil
- Pepper, use the Black

Procedure step by step:

1. Air fryer set to 180 degrees Celsius. Spray the fryer basket.
2. Cornflour, rice flour, salt, spices should be mixed and well combined.
3. Cover tofu with the flour mixture in a uniform manner and then sprinkle with olive oil.
4. Put tofu inside the basket and allow them to cook for about 28mins.
5. Transfer the tofu to a serving tray, and serve while it is still warm.

Dietary composition:
Calories: 249, Total fat: 16.5g, Sodium: 46mg, Carbs: 16.5g, Fiber: 1g, Protein: 9g

36. Tofu in Sweet and Spicy Sauce

Preparing time: 15 minutes
Time needed to cook: 6 minutes
Number of portions: 2

Required Material:

- 1 block 396 g) firm tofu, pressed and cubed
- 65 g arrowroot flour
- 2 scallions: green part), chopped
- ½ tsp sesame oil
- (Low-sodium) soy sauce: 4 Tbsp
- 1 and a half tbsp each: chili sauce, rice vinegar
- A single tbsp agave nectar
- Two large garlic cloves
- A tsp ginger, preferably fresh

Procedure step by step:

1. Combine tofu, arrowroot flour, and sesame oil in a bowl.
2. Transfer the all in an oiled basket. Cook

tofu for 20 mins
3. to 180°F in a fryer already warm.
4. In a bowl, unite all ingredients except scallions to form a sauce.
5. Amalgamate tofu and sauce in a pan for 3 minutes, stirring regularly.
6. Serve hot with scallion greens.

Dietary composition:
Calories: 348, Total fat: 10.5g, Sodium: 1589mg,
Carbs: 49g, Fiber: 3g, Protein: 15g,

37. Lemon Garlic Shrimps

Preparing time: 15 minutes
Time needed to cook: 8 minutes
Number of portions: 2

Required Material:

- 340g deveined shrimp
- 1½ tbsp only juice of lemon
- A tbsp olive oil
- Lemon pepper, a pinch
- ¼ tsp paprika
- ¼ tsp garlic in powder

Procedure step by step:

1. Warm the fryer to 200°C and oil the basket.
2. Combine lemon juice, olive oil, lemon pepper, paprika, and garlic powder.
3. Add shrimp and mix thoroughly.
4. Put the shrimp inside the air fryer basket and fry (8 mins.).
5. Serve shrimp warm on platters.

Dietary composition:
Calories: 173, Fat: 8g, Carbohydrates: 3g, Sugar: 0g, Protein: 23g, Sodium: 326mg

38. Creamy Tuna Cakes

Preparing time: 15 minutes
Time needed to cook: 15 minutes
Number of portions: 4

Required Material:

- 2 (340g) cans of tuna, drained
- 1½ TBSP almond flour
- 1½ TBSPs mayonnaise
- A tbsp only juice of lemon
- Two tsps dill and garlic powder (one of each)
- Half Tsp onion

- Pinch of salt
- Use Black pepper, as preferred

Procedure step by step:
1. Oil the Air fryer pan after starting your fryer. Temperature 200 degrees C.
2. Combine tuna, mayonnaise, wheat flour, lemon juice, dill, and spices.
3. Form the mixture into 4 burgers and put them in the basket.
4. Let it cook for about 12 mins, then turn them over.
5. Proceed for another 5 minutes, then put the tuna cakes on plates and serve them warm.

Dietary composition:
Calories: 103, Fat: 6.6g, Carbohydrates: 1.2g, Sugar: 0.1g, Protein: 9.2g, Sodium: 227.5mg

39. Cheesy Shrimp

Preparing time: 20 minutes
Time needed to cook: 20 minutes
Number of portions: 4

Required Material:
- 63g Parmesan cheese, grated
- 907g Peeled - deveined shrimp
- 4 grated garlic smashed
- 2 TBSPs EVO oil
- About one tsp dried basil
- A little oregano
- One single onion in powder
- Red pepper flakes, equaling half a tsp
- Black pepper Ground, as required
- Fresh lemon juice, need Two tbsp

Procedure step by step:
1. First, get an Air fryer basket ready greasing it, and start the fryer to 175 degrees C.
2. Combine the Parmesan cheese, garlic, oil, herbs, spices.
3. Cook shrimp for around 10 minutes by layering half of them in the basket.

4. When ready to serve, divide the shrimp among dishes and squeeze fresh lemon juice over them.

Dietary composition:
Calories: 399, Fat: 18g, Carbohydrates: 6g, Sugar: 1g, Protein: 47g, Sodium: 1296mg

40. Creamy Breaded Shrimp

Preparing time: 15 minutes
Time needed to cook: 20 minutes
Number of portions: 3

Required Material:
- 30g all-purpose flour
- 50g panko breadcrumbs
- 454g shrimp, peeled and deveined
- 120ml mayonnaise
- 60ml sweet chili sauce
- 1 TBSP Sriracha sauce

Procedure step by step:
1. Warm the air fryer to 200°C and oil the basket.
2. Put flour in a wide bowl and combine mayonnaise, chili sauce, and Sriracha sauce in another. Prepare a third dish of breadcrumbs.
3. Use them to coat each shrimp first in flour, then mayonnaise, and finally breadcrumbs.
4. After coating half of the shrimp, fry them for 10 mins in your A.Fryer.
5. When is all ready to serve, lay the shrimp on a platter and have fun!.

Dietary composition:
Calories: 637, Fat: 34g, Carbs: 45g, Sugar: 16g, Protein: 39g, Sodium: 1613mg

41. Breaded Shrimp with Lemon

Preparing time: 15 minutes
Time needed to cook: 14 minutes
Number of portions: 3

Required Material:

- 60g plain flour
- 2 egg whites
- 50g breadcrumbs
- 454g large shrimp
- A quarter Tsp (each): red pepper flakes, lemon zest, cayenne pepper
- 2 tbsp oil, type vegetable

Procedure step by step:

1. To start you need 3 dishes, then turn on the air fryer (200°C).
2. In the first dish combine flour, salt, and pepper.
3. Whisk egg whites in a second dish and combine breadcrumbs, lime zest, and spices in a third.
4. Dredge each shrimp in flour, then egg whites then breadcrumbs.
5. Sprinkle the shrimp with olive oil and use a greased basket to cook.
6. Insert in the fryer. After 7 minutes, platter the coated shrimp. Repeat with the rest. Serve.

Dietary composition:
Calories: 434, Fat: 13g, Carbohydrates: 43g, Sugar: 2g, Protein: 35g, Sodium: 739mg

42. Coconut Crusted Shrimp

Preparing time: 15 minutes
Time needed to cook: 40 minutes
Number of portions: 3

Required Material:

- 240ml coconut milk
- 40g sweetened coconut, shredded
- 25g panko breadcrumbs
- 454g (deveined) large shrimp
- Salt & black pepper, as preferred

Procedure step by step:

1. First, get an Air fryer basket ready greasing it.
2. Second, on a wide, shallow dish, pour the

milk from a coconut.

3. Inside a separate bowl, combine coconut, salt, breadcrumbs, black pepper.
4. Afterward, drench shrimp with the coconut milk and then the coconut crumbs.
5. Lay half the shrimp in your Air fryer and cook them (175°C - Twenty Mins.).
6. Distribute the shrimp among the plates, then serve the rest of the mixture in the same manner.

Dietary composition:
Calories: 449, Fats: 22g, Carbohydrates: 28g, Sugar: 10g, Proteins: 33g, Sodium: 675mg

43. Rice Flour Coated Shrimp

Preparing time: 20 minutes
Time needed to cook: 20 minutes
Number of portions: 3

Required Material:

- 3 TBSPs rice flour
- One pound shrimp
- 2 tbsp EVO oil
- Powdered sugar, a pinch
- Salt and (type black) pepper, as required

Procedure step by step:

1. First, lubricate an Air fryer basket and preheat the appliance to 163 degrees C.
2. Unite rice flour, olive oil, sugar, salt, and pepper.
3. Now include the shrimp by stirring them in, and then placing half of them in the fryer basket.
4. Prepare (10 minutes), turning once.
5. Transfer the mixture to serving dishes and repeat with the leftovers.

Dietary composition:
Calories: 241, Fat: 9.5g, Sodium: 451mg, Protein: 30.7g, Carbs: 7.4g, Sugar: 1.5g

44. Shrimp Kebabs

Preparing time: 15 minutes
Time needed to cook: 10 minutes
Number of portions: 2

Required Material:

- 340g shrimp
- A tbsp fresh cilantro
- Wooden skewers, presoaked
- 2 tbsp only lemon juice fresh
- One small garlic, minced
- ½ tsp Paprika
- ½ tsp ground cumin
- Spices, as required

Procedure step by step:

1. Initialize your air fryer to 175°C and spray basket with a little oil.
2. Combine lemon juice, garlic, and seasonings. Stir shrimp.
3. Arrange shrimp on presoaked skewers and lay in a basket.
4. Let it prepare for 10 minutes, rotating halfway.
5. Served with fresh cilantro.

Dietary composition:
Calories: 130, Fat: 2.5g, Carbohydrates: 3g, Sugar: 0.5g, Protein: 23g, Sodium: 240mg

45. Garlic Parmesan Shrimp

Preparing time: 20 minutes
Time needed to cook: 10 minutes
Number of portions: 2

Required Material:

- 454g shrimp, deveined and peeled
- 50g parmesan cheese, grated
- 15g cilantro, diced
- Obtain two TBSPs by mixing olive oil and lemon juice
- A dash salt
- Cracked pepper, one tsp

- 6 garlic cloves, diced

Procedure step by step:

1. The temperature of the air fryer reaches 175 degrees Celsius.
2. Oil a basket that fits inside the air fryer.
3. Sprinkle the shrimp with mix oil-lemon, garlic, spices.
4. Wrap the bowl with plastic wrap, place it in the refrigerator for about three hours.
5. Add the grated parmesan cheese and chopped cilantro to the bowl, then transfer the mixture to the basket of an air fryer.
6. Prepared food should be served soon after ten minutes cook.

Dietary composition:
Calories: 342, Fat: 16g, Carbohydrates: 5g, Sugar: 1g, Protein: 44g, Sodium: 2006mg

46. Prawn Burgers

Preparing time: 20 minutes
Time needed to cook: 6 minutes
Number of portions: 2

Required Material:

- 120g prawns, peeled, deveined, and finely chopped
- 60g breadcrumbs
- 2-3 TBSPs onion, finely chopped
- 450g fresh baby greens
- Half tsp of each spices (Chili red, garlic, turmeric, ginger, cumin)
- Salt & (ground black) pepper, as required

Procedure step by step:

1. Set the air fryer to 200 degrees Celsius and oil a basket that fits inside your fryer
2. Combine prawns, breadcrumbs, onion, ginger, garlic, and spices.
3. Form the mixture into a number of patties of varying sizes.
4. Allow to cook, approximately six mins, then transfer to a serving tray.
5. Serve immediately, while still heated,

together with the young greens.

Dietary composition:
Calories: 221, Fat: 4g, Carbohydrates: 29g, Sugar: 2g, Protein: 18g, Sodium: 432mg

47. Black Sea Bass with Rosemary Vinaigrette

Preparing time: 17 minutes
Number of portions: 4

Required Material:
- 4 black sea bass fillets; boneless and skin scored
- 3 minced garlic cloves
- Two tbsp. olive oil
- A tbsp. Rosemary
- Three tbsp. black olives
- Salt, Juice of 1 lime, pepper

Procedure step by step:
1. Mix the other ingredients (save the fish) with the olive oil in a bowl first, then add the fish.
2. Then, lay the fish in an air fryer-friendly pan and drizzle the whole thing with the rosemary dressing.
3. Put the pan in a preheated 193°C oven for 12 minutes, flipping the fish over halfway through cooking. Divide among platters and serve.

Dietary composition:
Calories: 258, Fat: 14.8g, Chol.: 101mg, Sodium: 167mg, Carbohydrates: 2.4g, Fiber: 0.8g, Sugars: 0.3g, Protein: 28.4g

48. Tuna Zoodle Casserole

Preparing time: 30 minutes
Number of portions: 4

Required Material:
- 28 g pork rinds, finely ground
- 2 medium zucchini, spiralized
- 2 cans (500 g) albacore tuna

- 40 g diced white onion
- 30 g chopped white mushrooms
- 2 stalks celery, finely chopped
- 120 ml heavy cream
- 120 ml vegetable broth
- 2 tbsp. full-fat mayonnaise
- 2 tbsp. salted butter
- ½ tsp. red pepper flakes
- ¼ tsp. xanthan gum

Procedure step by step:
1. Melt butter in a big saucepan. Sauté onion, mushrooms, and celery 3–5 minutes.
2. Add heavy cream, vegetable broth, mayonnaise, and xanthan gum. Boil lightly for 3 minutes till the mixture thickens.
3. Zucchini, tuna, and red pepper flakes. Off heat, toss zucchini noodles until covered. Fill a round baking dish.
4. Lay ground pork rinds and position a foil on the basket of the Air F. Cook after actuating the timer for 15 minutes at 187 degrees C.
5. Eliminate the foil after 3 minutes to brown the casserole. Serve hot.

Dietary composition:
Calories: 419, Fat: 33.6g, Saturated Fat: 18.4g, Cholesterol: 140mg, Sodium: 697mg, Carbohydrates: 5.4g, Fiber: 1.2g, Sugars: 2.6g, Protein: 25.6g

49. Spicy Avocado Cod

Preparing time: 20 minutes
- Number of portions: 2

Required Material:
- 1 medium avocado; peeled, pitted and sliced
- 60 ml chopped pickled jalapeños.
- 2 (170 g).cod fillets
- ½ medium lime
- 70 g shredded cabbage

- 60 ml sour cream, full-fat.
- Mayonnaise, type full-fat 2 tbsp.
- ½ tsp. paprika
- Garlic ¼ tsp.
- A tsp. chili powder plus cumin

Procedure step by step:

1. Combine cabbage, sour cream, mayonnaise, and jalapeños. Coat thoroughly. Refrigerate 20 minutes.
2. Season cod fillets with chile, cumin, paprika, and garlic powder. Air-fried each fillet. Set the timer for 10 minutes at 187 degrees C.
3. Turn fillets halfway through cooking. Fish should be cooked to 62 degrees C.
4. Distribute slaw mixture into two bowls, break fish fillets into pieces, and top with avocado. Lime juice in each bowl. Serve.

Dietary composition:
Calories: 413, Fat: 32g, Protein: 22g,
Carbohydrates: 12g, Fiber: 7g

50. E-Z Catfish

Preparing time: 15 minutes
Number of portions: 3

Required Material:

- Olive oil: 1 tbsp.
- Seasoned fish fry: 50 g
- Catfish fillets: 4

Procedure step by step:

1. Pre-heat your fryer to 200°C. Rinse and dry the fish.
2. Pour seasoning into a large zip-top bag. Shake fish fillets. Sprinkle Cooking oil spray.
3. Insert the pan, set 10 mins of the clock to cook. Turn and add 10 minutes. Rotate again and cook for 2–3 minutes.
4. Put it on a plate when it is crunchy.

Dietary composition:
Calories: 341, Fat: 16 g, Sodium: 509 mg, Chol: 89 mg, Carbohydrates: 10 g, Protein: 38 g,

51. Fish & Chips

Preparing time: 10 minutes
Number of portions: 4

Required Material:

- Catfish fillets or similar fish: 2
- Wholemeal bread for breadcrumbs: 3 slices
- Medium beaten egg: 1
- Bag tortilla chips: 25g
- Juice and rind of 1 lemon
- Pepper and salt
- Parsley: 1 tbsp.

Procedure step by step:

1. Pre-heat the fryer to 180o Celsius.
2. Lemon zest and juice.
3. Cut the fillets into four cooking pieces. Lemon juice for each one fillet and set away.
4. Combine tortilla chips, parsley, pepper, breadcrumbs, and lemon zest in a food processor.
5. Wash fish and beat egg. Pass in the crumb mixture. Bake till crispy.
6. Getting ready takes ten minutes and cooking takes fifteen, so be patient and wait.

Dietary composition
Calories: 394, Fat: 14 g, Cholesterol: 159 mg, Carbs: 24 g, Sugar: 1 g, Sodium: 385 mg, Protein: 42 g, Fiber: 2 g

52. Buttered Crab Shells

Preparing time: 20 minutes
Time needed to cook: 10 minutes
Number of portions: 4

Required Material:

- Soft crab shells, cleaned: 4
- 240 ml butter-milk
- Eggs: 3
- 240 g breadcrumb, panko
- 2 TBSPs butter, melted

- 2 tsp seasoning of seafood
- A quarter grated lemon zest

Procedure step by step:

1. Oil the basket and turn on the air fryer to 190°C.
2. Beat the eggs and buttermilk in separate bowls.
3. Combine breadcrumbs, seafood seasoning, and lemon zest in a third bowl.
4. Immerse crab shells in eggs after soaking them in buttermilk for 10 minutes.
5. Dip in breadcrumbs and place crab shells in the Air fryer basket.
6. Serve with melted butter after 10 minutes cook.

Dietary composition:

Calories: 466, Fat: 16 g, Saturated Fat: 7 g, Cholesterol: 239 mg, Carbohydrates: 51 g, Fiber: 2 g, Sugar: 7 g, Protein: 29 g, Sodium: 936 mg

53. Pesto Salmon

Preparing time: 10 minutes
Time needed to cook: 16 minutes
Serve: 4

Required Material:

- 700 g salmon fillet
- 1 tbsp green pesto
- 240 ml mayonnaise
- 15 ml olive oil
- 450 g fresh spinach
- 57 g parmesan cheese, grated
- Pepper
- Salt

Procedure step by step:

1. First, get the air fryer up to temperature of 190 degrees C.
2. Use cooking spray to coat the air fryer's basket.
3. Third, place salmon in basket and season them with spices.
4. Combine mayonnaise, parmesan, and

pesto in a bowl, then distribute it over the salmon fillet. Salmon needs to be cooked for 14-16 minutes.
5. While that is happening, sauté some spinach in olive oil for two to three minutes, or until it wilts. Sprinkle with salt & pepper.
6. Place fresh spinach on a plate to serve and then top with the salmon that has been cooked. Eat up!.

Dietary composition:

Calories: 714kcal, Fat: 59g, Sodium: 862mg, Chol: 142mg, Carbs: 9g, Sugar: 2g, Fiber: 4g, Protein: 38g

54. Honey & Sriracha Tossed Calamari

Preparing time: 25 minutes
Number of portions: 1-2

Required Material:

- Calamari tubes - tentacles if you prefer: 300 g
- Club soda: 240 ml
- Flour: 120 g
- Salt - red pepper & black pepper: 2 dashes each
- Honey: 120 ml + 1-2 tbsp. Sriracha
- Red pepper flakes: 2 shakes

Procedure step by step:

1. Wash and dry the calamari with paper towels. Cut into rings. Throw rings into a dish. Stir in club soda. 10-minute wait.
2. Sift salt, flour, red, and black pepper.
3. Dredge the calamari in flour and lay it on a tray until frying.
4. Lightly spray the Air Fryer basket with cooking oil. Avoid crowding the basket with calamari.
5. Set your fryer to 190°C and 11 minutes.
6. Shake the basket twice during cooking to separate the rings.
7. Take off from basket, stir with sauce, and cook for two more minutes. Add other

sauce as needed.

8. Mix honey, sriracha, and red pepper flakes to make the sauce for serving.

Dietary composition:
Calories: 573, Total fat: 11g, Sugars: 27g, Chol: 834mg, Sodium: 2696mg, Carbs: 55g, Fiber: 1g, Protein: 64g

55. Bacon Wrapped Scallops

Preparing time: 15 minutes
Time needed to cook: 12 minutes
Number of portions: 4

Required Material:

- 5 center-cut bacon slices, cut each into 4 pieces
- 20 sea scallops, cleaned and patted very dry
- Olive oil cooking spray
- 1 tsp lemon pepper seasoning
- ½ tsp paprika
- Salt & ground black pepper, as preferred

Procedure step by step:

1. First, have an Air fryer basket ready and preheat the appliance to 200 degrees C.
2. Second, place a toothpick in the center of each bacon-wrapped scallop.
3. Lemon-pepper condiment and paprika should be sprinkled evenly over the scallops.
4. After spraying the Air fryer basket with cooking spray, place half of the scallops inside.
5. Five minutes later, season with salt and black pepper and take out of the frying.
6. Repeat with the second half and serve immediately while still hot.

Dietary composition:
Calories: 194, Fat: 9.3g, Carbs: 2.6g, Fiber: 0.1g, Protein: 24.4g, Cholesterol: 65mg, Sugar: 0.4g, Sodium: 477mg

56. Lemon Fish

Preparing time: 30 minutes
Number of portions: 4

Required Material:

- Water: 118 ml + 3 tbsp.
- Sugar: 60 g
- Juice of 1 lemon
- Green chili sauce: 2 tsp.
- Salt: to your liking
- Egg white: 1
- Corn flour slurry: 4 tsp.
- Red chili sauce: 1 tsp.
- Lettuce: 2-3 leaves
- Catfish: 2 - cut into 4 pieces
- Oil: 2 tsp.

Procedure step by step:

1. Water and sugar should boil. Lemon should be sliced and put on a plate.
2. Combine egg white, oil, chili sauce, salt, and flour in a bowl. Incorporate three TBSPs of water into a slurry batter.
3. Flour put on a plate. Dip fillets in batter then flour.
4. Spray cooking oil on the Air Fryer basket and heat to 180°C.
5. Cook the fillets in the basket for 15–20 minutes until crispy.
6. Stir salt and mix again together with corn flour slurry. Incorporate red sauce juice and lemon slices and simmer until thickened.
7. Take the fish from the basket, spray with oil, and put back in, just 5 mins.
8. Lay lettuce on a serving plate. Position the fish and garnish with the lemon sauce. Eat!.

Dietary composition:
Calories: 227, Fat: 7g, Carbs: 18g, Protein: 22g, Cholesterol: 61mg, Sodium: 442mg, Fiber: 1g, Sugar: 13g

57. Chicken with Veggies and Rice

Preparing time: 15 minutes
Time needed to cook: 20 minutes
Number of portions: 3

Required Material:

- 540g cold boiled white rice
- 150g chicken, already cooked
- 60g carrots
- 60g peas
- 80g onion
- 6 tbsp soy sauce
- A tbsp vegetable oil

Procedure step by step:

1. Turn on the Air fryer and pre-heat the pan to 182 degrees C with the nonstick surface.
2. Then, mix the rice, soy sauce, and vegetable oil together in a bowl.
3. Toss in the remaining ingredients, making sure they are well distributed.
4. The fryer is ready to receive the pan containing the rice mixture.
5. Get ready in 20 minutes and serve immediately.

Dietary composition:
Calories: 373, Fat: 9g, Carbohydrates: 53g, Sugar: 4g, Protein: 20g, Sodium: 1136mg

58. Delicious Chicken Burgers

Preparing time: 20 minutes
Time needed to cook: 30 minutes
Number of portions: 4

Required Material:

- 4 (680g) chicken breasts
- 50g flour
- Two eggs
- 4 toasted hamburger buns
- Four slices mozzarella cheese
- A tsp of: mustard powder, Worcestershire sauce, garlic, chicken seasoning
- Half tsp paprika plus Pepper of Cayenne
- Parsley, Oregano, Tarragon use all One tsp
- Spices, as required

Procedure step by step:

1. First, have a basket ready and preheat the appliance to 180 degrees C.
2. Mince the chicken breasts with the help of a food processor and the addition of mustard, paprika, Worcestershire sauce, salt, and black pepper.
3. Make four patties from the mixture.
4. To make the batter, whisk the egg in a separate bowl and then add the flour in a broad, shallow dish.
5. Combine the dry herbs and spices in a separate dish. The chicken patties are dusted of meal, dipped in the beaten egg, and then coated in the breadcrumb mixture.
6. Chicken patties should be fried in a single layer in a basket for 30 minutes, with the patties turned over once.
7. Arrange a lettuce leaf, burger patty, and cheese slice on half of the bread.
8. Serve warm, covering with the bun top

Dietary composition:
Calories: 487, Fat: 19g, Carbohydrates: 32g, Sugar: 3g, Protein: 44g, Sodium: 932mg

59. Simple Turkey Breast

Preparing time: 20 minutes
Time needed to cook: 40 minutes
Number of portions: 10

Required Material:

- 1 (3.6kg) bone-in turkey breast
- Salt & Pepper-Black, as required
- Olive oil, Two tbsp

Procedure step by step:

1. Set the temperature to 182 degrees C and grease a fry basket.
2. Add salt, pepper, and oil to the turkey breast.
3. Then, lay the turkey breasts in the A.F. basket skin-side down and cook for 20 minutes.
4. After the first 20 minutes, flip the meat and continue frying for another 20 minutes.
5. Spread it on a platter and cut into whichever many servings you choose.

Dietary composition:
Calories: 160, Fat: 5g, Carbohydrates: 0g, Sugar: 0g, Protein: 27g, Sodium: 87mg

60. Buttermilk Brined Turkey Breast

Preparing time: 15 minutes
Time needed to cook: 20 minutes
Number of portions: 8

Required Material:

- 177ml brine from a can of olives
- 1588g boneless, skinless turkey breast
- 2 sprigs of thyme
- A single sprig rosemary
- 118ml buttermilk

Procedure step by step:

1. First, have an Air fryer basket ready to go and preheat the appliance to 175 degrees C.
2. Second, combine the buttermilk and olive

brine in a basin.

3. In the reusable plastic bag put turkey breast, buttermilk mixture, and herb sprigs. Put the bag in the fridge for 12 hours, sealed.

4. Take the turkey breasts out of the package and place them in the Air fryer basket.

5. Cook for 20 minutes total, turning once.

6. When ready, lay the turkey breast on a chopping board, and slice it into serving-sized pieces before serving.

Dietary composition:
Calories: 228, Fat: 3.9g, Carbohydrates: 3.6g, Sugar: 3.6g, Protein: 43g, Sodium: 1251mg

61. Delightful Turkey Wings

Preparing time: 10 minutes
Time needed to cook: 26 minutes
Number of portions: 4

Required Material:
- 907g of turkey wings
- 4 TBSPs chicken rub
- 3 TBSPs olive oil

Procedure step by step:
1. Turn up the Air fryer to 193 degrees C and coat with oil the Air fryer pan.
2. Combine the turkey wings, chicken rub, and olive oil in a bowl.
3. Put the turkey wings in the basket of the Air fryer and roast for about 26 minutes, turning them over once.
4. Place the wings on a plate and serve them hot.

Dietary composition:
Calories: 370, Fat: 28g, Carbohydrates: 1g, Sugar: 0g, Protein: 28g, Sodium: 380mg

62. Duck Rolls

Preparing time: 20 minutes
Time needed to cook: 40 minutes
Number of portions: 3

Required Material:
- 454g duck breast fillet, each cut into 2 pieces
- Fresh and chopped Parsley: 3 Tbsp
- A small onion-red, plus one garlic
- 1 and ½ tsp cumin
- Cinnamon, a tsp
- Only Half tsp red chili powder
- Evo oil and salt

Procedure step by step:
1. Grease an air fryer basket and warm the device to 180 degrees Celsius.
2. Combine olive oil, garlic, parsley, onion, and spices.
3. Cut a horizontal incision through each piece of duck and sprinkle it with the onion mixture.
4. Roll each piece of duck firmly before placing it in the basket of the air fryer.
5. After 40 minutes of cooking, cut the meat into pieces of your choice to serve.

Dietary composition:
Calories: 380, Fats: 25g, Carbohydrates: 5g, Sugar: 1g, Proteins: 34g, Sodium: 290mg

63. Turkey Meatloaf

Preparing time: 20 minutes
Time needed to cook: 20 minutes
Number of portions: 4

Required Material:
- 454g ground turkey
- 160g kale leaves
- One onion
- 60g fresh breadcrumbs
- 120g Monterey Jack cheese, grated
- 2 garlic cloves, minced
- 60ml salsa verde
- A tsp red chili powder
- One TSP cumin plus oregano
- Salt & pepper-Black, as required

Procedure step by step:

1. To begin, preheat the A.Fryer to 200 °C and oil the basket.
2. Divide the turkey mixture into four portions, then mix all the ingredients together.
3. Third, shape each into a little loaf, and set the basket in the fryer.
4. After 20 minutes of cooking, serve.

Dietary composition:
Calories: 370, Fat: 20g, Carbohydrates: 14g, Sugar: 4g, Protein: 33g, Sodium: 530mg

64. Buttered Duck Breasts

Preparing time: 15 minutes
Time needed to cook: 22 minutes
Number of portions: 4

Required Material:

- 2: 340g duck breasts
- Butter, Three Tbsp
- Salt of sea
- Half tsp crushed thyme
- 1-quarter tsp star anise
- Black pepper

Procedure step by step:

1. Add a lot of spices to the duck breasts.
2. Put the meat in the oiled A.F. basket and cook for about 10 mins at a temperature of 200°C.
3. Take off the duck breasts and pour the melted butter over them, thyme, and star anise powder:
4. Put them back to cook more (12 minutes). It's ready.

Dietary composition:
Calories: 380, Fat: 29g, Carbohydrates: 0g, Sugar: 0g, Protein: 29g, Sodium: 280mg

65. Beer Coated Duck Breast

Preparing time: 15mins.
Time needed to cook: 20 minutes
Number of portions: 2

Required Material:

- 1 TBSP fresh thyme, chopped
- 240ml beer
- 1 (298g) duck breast
- 6 cherry tomatoes
- 1 TBSP EVO oil
- Mustard, one tsp
- Salt + Pepper, as required
- Balsamic vinegar

Procedure step by step:

1. Oil a fryer basket. The Air Fryer temperature should reach 200°C.
2. Then, in a separate bowl, whip together the olive oil, mustard, thyme, beer, and spices.
3. Marinate duck breasts in the mixture for four hours, then add them.
4. Cook the duck breasts in your fryer for 15 minutes after placing them in a foil-lined basket.
5. Eliminate the foil and lower the temperature to 185 degrees C; add the duck breast and tomatoes.
6. Serve duck breasts and cherry tomatoes after 5 minutes together a vinegar-drizzled.

Dietary composition:
Calories: 371, Fat: 20.5g, Carbohydrates: 7.6g, Sugar: 3.1g, Protein: 29.3g, Sodium: 191mg

66. Duck Breast with Figs

Preparing time: 20 minutes
Time needed to cook: 45 minutes
Number of portions: 2

Required Material:

- 454g duck breast only boneless

- 6 (360g) figs fresh
- 1 TBSP fresh thyme, chopped
- 480ml juice pomegranate
- 2 tbsp lemon juice
- Three tbsp brown sugar
- Evo oil and spices, as required

Procedure step by step:
1. Warm the air fryer to 200 degrees C and oil the basket.
2. Mix equal parts juice (lemon and pomegranate) with brown sugar. Let it lightly boil inside a sauce-pan for around 25 mins.
3. Season the duck breasts heavily with salt and pepper.
4. Cook the duck breasts in the Air fryer for 14 minutes with the skin side up, turning once.
5. Put them on a cutting board and wait 10 minutes.
6. To make the fig salad, combine figs, oil, spices in the basket of your A.Fryer and set the timer for 5 minutes.
7. Irrorate the heated pomegranate juice with the duck breast and toasted figs. Up a little fresh thyme and serve hot.

Dietary composition:
Calories: 615, Fat: 29g, Carbohydrates: 45g, Sugar: 38g, Protein: 44g, Sodium: 311mg

67. Asian Style Chicken

Preparing time: 40 minutes
Number of portions: 4

Required Material:
- 454 g. spinach; chopped.
- 680 g. chicken drumsticks
- 425 ml canned tomatoes; crushed
- 60 ml lemon juice
- 120 ml chicken stock
- 120 ml heavy cream
- 120 ml cilantro; chopped.

- 4 garlic cloves
- A yellow onion.
- 2 tbsp. loosed butter
- 1 tbsp. ginger; grated
- 1 and ½ tsp. of coriander, paprika
- One tsp. turmeric powder
- Salt & pepper, as prefer

Procedure step by step:
1. In a suitable pan for your A.Fryer, melt the butter.
2. Mix in the garlic, onion, and other fragrant herbs and spices. Cook for 3 minutes often stirring.
3. Chicken and tomatoes continue cooking for another 4 minutes, after adding.
4. Toss in the broth and then place the pan in the deep fryer. (20 mins at 187 degrees C).
5. Just five minutes before the end of cooking, combine the spinach, lemon juice, cilantro, and cream. Give each person their own bowl and dig in.

Dietary composition:
Calories: 466, Fat: 28g, Saturated Fat: 12g, Cholesterol: 199mg, Sodium: 471mg, Carbohydrates: 14g, Fiber: 4g, Sugar: 5g, Protein: 43g

68. Lemongrass Chicken

Preparing time: 40 minutes
Number of portions: 4

Required Material:
- 10 chicken drumsticks
- 236 ml coconut milk
- 1 bunch lemongrass; trimmed
- 15 g parsley; chopped.
- 1 yellow onion; chopped.
- A total 6 tbsp of fish and soy sauce
- Butter, a tsp
- Ginger the quantity of a tbsp.
- 4 garlic
- A tbsp. lemon juice

- Salt and Pepper-Black

Procedure step by step:

1. Use a food processor to thoroughly combine the lemongrass, ginger, garlic, soy sauce, fish sauce, and coconut milk.

2. Start by melting the butter in a dish that can go in your air fryer. The onions should be added and cooked for three minutes.

3. Mix the lemongrass paste, salt, and pepper into the chicken, then combine the two mixtures in a bowl.

4. To deep fry the contents of the pan, pour them in at a temperature of 193°C for 25 minutes.

5. Combine the lemon juice with the chopped parsley. Plating and serving everything is a must.

Dietary composition:
Calories: 414, Fat: 27g, Saturated Fat: 14g, Cholesterol: 132mg, Sodium: 1294mg, Carbohydrates: 10g, Fiber: 2g, Sugar: 3g, Protein: 33g

69. Chicken and Chickpeas

Preparing time: 35 minutes
Number of portions: 4

Required Material:

- 907 g chicken thighs; boneless
- 227 g canned chickpeas; drained
- 142 g bacon; cooked and crumbled
- 236 ml chicken stock
- 1 tsp. balsamic v*inegar
- Two tbsp. EVO oil
- 240 g onion
- 2 carrots
- A tbsp. parsley
- Salt & Pepper

Procedure step by step:

1. First, heat the oil in a pan that may fit into your air fryer.

2. Stirring periodically, sauté the onions, carrots, spices for three to four minutes.

3. Third, combine the chicken and chickpeas with the stock and vinegar.

4. Set oven temperature to 193 degrees - 20 mins.

5. Throw in the bacon and parsley. Distribute the food among the plates.

Dietary composition:
Calories: 580 kcal, Fat: 37g, Carbohydrates: 15g, Fiber: 3g, Protein: 46g

70. Pickle Fried Chicken

Time needed to cook: 47 minutes
Number of portions: 4

Required Material:

- 4 chicken legs; bone-in, skin on, cut into drumsticks and thighs, about 1600 g.
- 2 eggs
- 56.7 g almond flour
- Pickle juice from 680 g of kosher dill pickles
- 128 g breadcrumbs
- 1 tsp. black pepper
- 1 tsp. sea salt
- 2 tbsp. olive oil
- 1/8 tsp. cayenne pepper
- 1/2 tsp. ground paprika

Procedure step by step:

1. Pour pickle juice over the chicken. Cover and refrigerate chicken in pickle juice for 8 hours.

2. Remove chicken from fridge. Salt and pepper flour in a bowl. Whisk egg and olive oil in another basin.

3. Combine breadcrumbs, paprika, salt, pepper, and cayenne pepper in a third bowl. Air fryer to 187°C. Dry the chicken.

4. Flour, egg, and breadcrumb coats chicken pieces. Lay each piece of breaded chicken on a baking sheet. Air-fry chicken twice.

5. Put two thighs and two drumsticks in the fryer. Ten-minute air fry. Flip chicken and cook another 10 minutes.

6. Set chicken aside. Repeat with the second chicken batch. Lower to 170°C.

7. Air-fried the first batch of chicken on top of the second for 7 minutes.

Dietary composition:
Calories: 615 kcal, Fat: 38 g, Protein: 53 g, Carbohydrates: 16 g, Fiber: 2 g, Sugar: 5 g, Sodium: 2480 mg

71. Spicy Buffalo Wings

Time needed to cook: 26 minutes
Number of portions: 4

Required Material:

- 907 g chicken wings
- 120 ml hot & spicy sauce; divided
- 6 tbsp. melted butter; divided
- Salt to taste

Procedure step by step:

1. Mix 60 ml hot and spicy sauce and 44 ml melted butter in a bowl. Cover chicken pieces with marinade and marinate in the fridge for 2 hours.

2. Warm air-fryer to 200°C. Two batches of wings. Air fry the first batch for 12 minutes, shaking halfway through.

3. Fry the second, then put all wings for another 2 minutes to fry.

4. Mix the remaining 44 ml butter and 60 ml hot sauce to finish. Enjoy sauced wings!

Dietary composition:
Calories: 486, Fat: 39g, Saturated Fat: 16g, Cholesterol: 171mg, Sodium: 940mg, Carbohydrates: 2g, Sugar: 2g, Protein: 31g

72. Crunchy Chicken Strips

Time needed to cook: 12 minutes
Number of portions: 8

Required Material:

- 1 chicken breast; cut into strips
- 110 g breadcrumbs
- 30g almond flour
- 1 egg; beaten

- 1 tsp. mix spice
- 1 tbsp. plain oats
- 1 tbsp. dried coconut
- Salt and pepper to taste

Procedure step by step:

1. In a bowl, mix oats, mix spice, coconut, pepper, salt, and breadcrumbs. Add beaten egg to another bowl. Add the flour to a third dish

2. Take the flour and coat chicken strips with it, then dip in egg and roll in breadcrumb mixture. Place the coated chicken strips in the air fryer basket and air fry at 180°C and cook for 4 minutes. Serve hot!

Dietary composition:
Calories: 107, Fat: 4g, Saturated Fat: 1g, Cholesterol: 33mg, Sodium: 180mg, Carbohydrates: 11g, Fiber: 1g, Sugar: 1g, Protein: 8g

73. Teriyaki Chicken

Time needed to cook: 14 minutes
Number of portions: 2

Required Material:

- 2 boneless; skinless chicken thighs
- 1 tsp. ginger; grated.
- 3 tbsp. teriyaki sauce
- 1 tbsp. cooking wine

Procedure step by step:

1. First, combine everything in a bowl. Cool for 30 minutes in the fridge before use.

2. Put the marinated chicken in an air fryer pan and bake it at 180 degrees Celsius for 8 minutes.

3. Turn the chicken over after 8 minutes and cook for another 6 minutes. Ready to be eaten up hot.

Dietary composition:
Calories: 209, Fat: 8g, Saturated Fat: 2g, Cholesterol: 107mg, Sodium: 1043mg, Carbohydrates: 8g, Sugar: 7g, Protein: 24g

74. Crispy Honey Chicken Wings

Time needed to cook: 35 minutes
Number of portions: 8

Required Material:

- 16 pieces chicken wings
- 60 ml clover honey
- 30 ml water; or as needed
- 110 g potato starch
- 55 g butter
- 4 tbsp. garlic; minced
- 1/2 tsp. kosher salt

Procedure step by step:

1. Wash and dry chicken wings and combine them with potato starch. Air fry wings at 190°C for 25 minutes, shaking the basket every five.
2. Cook at 200°C for 5-10 minutes afterward. All wings should have dry, crisp skin.
3. Low-heat a small stainless steel pot. Garlic sauté in melted butter 5-minute. Add salt and honey.
4. Simmer on low for 20 minutes, stirring occasionally. After 15 minutes, add a few drops of water to prevent sauce hardening.
5. Pour sauce over chicken wings after air-frying. Serve.

Dietary composition:
Calories: 372, Fat: 20g, Saturated Fat: 8g, Cholesterol: 111mg, Sodium: 343mg, Carbohydrates: 23g, Sugar: 10g, Protein: 24g

75. Meatloaf

Preparing time: 10 minutes
Time needed to cook: 28 minutes
Serve: 8

Required Material:

- 1 egg
- Chili, garlic a tsp of each
- 908 g ground turkey

- 57 g BBQ sauce, sugar-free
- 1 tsp ground mustard
- 1 tbsp onion, minced
- 113 g cheddar cheese, shredded
- 1 tsp salt

Procedure step by step:

1. First, get the air fryer up to 190 degrees Fahrenheit temperature.
2. Assemble all components in a single bowl before transferring them to the silicon loaf pan.
3. Third, cook the loaves in the air fryer for 25-28 minutes, using the loaf pan.
4. Dish Out and Savor.

Dietary composition:
Calories: 254 kcal, Fat: 14 g, Saturated Fat: 6 g, Carbohydrates: 4 g, Fiber: 1 g, Sugar: 1 g, Protein: 27 g, Sodium: 539 mg

76. Chicken Sandwich

Time needed to cook: 16 minutes
Number of portions: 2

Required Material:

- 2 chicken breasts; boneless and skinless
- 2 eggs
- 4 hamburger buns; buttered or toasted
- 8 dill pickle chips
- 118 ml dill pickle juice
- 118 ml milk
- 120 g flour, alle-use
- Two tbsp. Sugar
- Salt and paprika a pinch
- Half tsp pepper, . garlic, celery seed
- 1 tbsp. EVO oil

Procedure step by step:

1. Insert the chicken in a Ziploc bag and pound it to a thickness of half an inch. Then, depending on how big the chicken is, cut it into two to three pieces.
2. Then, put the chicken back in the Ziploc

bag and add pickle juice. Marinate in the fridge for at least half an hour.

3. Mix eggs and milk together. Then, incorporate flour, sugar, and spices together in another bowl.

4. Pass the chicken through both mixtures. Get rid of the extra.

5. Spray olive oil in A.F. tin and add the chicken. Also, oil the chicken and cook it at 170°C for 6 minutes.

6. Turn the chicken over and spray the other side with oil. Cook for another 6 minutes.

7. (To 200°C) cook each side for 2 minutes. Then, serve with pickle chips on buns that have been buttered and toasted.

Dietary composition:

Calories: 680kcal, Protein: 58g, Fat: 27g, Saturated Fat: 6g, Carbohydrates: 51g, Fiber: 2g, Sugar: 10g, Cholesterol: 337mg, Sodium: 1930mg

77. Pork Chops in Yogurt Sauce

Preparing time: 10 mins
Time needed to cook: 30 minutes
Number of portions: 4

Required Material:
- 2 tbsp oil of avocado
- 908g pork chops
- 240ml yogurt
- 2 garlic
- Turmeric powder, a pinch
- 2 TBSP oregano

Procedure step by step:
1. Simply combine the pork chops, yogurt, and remaining ingredients in the A.F. pan, toss, and prepare at 200 degrees C for 30 mins.
2. Then, put the mixture evenly among plates for serving.

Dietary composition:
Calories 209, Fat 12,5g, Fiber 0g, Carbs 3g, Protein 20g

78. Lamb Stew

Preparing time: 10 minutes
Time needed to cook: 35 minutes
Number of portions: 5-6

Required Material:
- 908g of diced lamb stew meat
- 900g acorn squash
- 4 Medium carrots
- 2 Small yellow onions
- 2 Rosemary Sprigs.

- 1 bay leaf
- 6 sliced or minced cloves of garlic
- 3 Tbsp of broth or water
- ¼ Tbsp of sp salt (Adjust it to taste)

Procedure step by step:
1. Remove peel and seed your acorn squash, then cut it into cubes. You can cook the squash in the microwave for 2 minutes, which is a good trick.
2. Cut the carrots into circles that are about an inch thick.
3. Peel your onions, cut them in half, and then cut them into half-moon shapes.
4. Using the Soup/Stew function is a good way to cook your soup, pressing the button after combining ingredients.
5. Set the timer for 35 minutes and close the lid.
6. When the timer beeps off, let the pressure and steam out before you open the lid.
7. Eat the stew!

Dietary composition:
Calories: 365, Protein: 36g. Fat: 18g. Carbs: 16g.

79. Lamb & Macadamia Nuts Mix

Preparing time: 10mins
Time needed to cook: 20 minutes
Number of portions: 4

Required Material:
- 907g lamb stew meat
- 20g macadamia Nuts
- 38g spinach
- 120ml stock of beef
- Garlic, two
- 3g oregano

Procedure step by step:
1. After being mixed with nuts and spices, roast lamb for twenty minutes at a temperature of 190 degrees Celsius, then served.

Dietary composition:
Calories 280, Fat 12, Fiber 8, Carbs 20, Protein 19

80. Beef with Cucumber & Eggplants

Preparing time: 10 minutes
Time needed to cook: 20 minutes
Number of portions: 4

Required Material:
- 454g beef meat for stew
- Two pieces of each eggplants, cucumbers, garlic
- 240ml cream, heavy
- EVO oil, Two Tbsp
- Salt and black pepper to the taste

Procedure step by step:
1. Using a baking dish that is appropriate for your air fryer, add the meat, veggies, and any other ingredients and then toss to mix everything well.
2. Place the pan into the fryer and set the temperature to 200 degrees Celsius. Cook for twenty minutes.
3. Place the meal in individual bowls and serve it.

Dietary composition:
Calories 484, Tot Fat 40, Fiber 4, Carbs 12, Sugar 5g, Protein 21g

81. Rosemary Pork and Artichokes

Preparing time: 10 minutes
Time needed to cook: 25 minutes
Number of portions: 4

Required Material:
- 454g pork stew meat, cubed
- 240g canned artichoke hearts, drained and halved
- 2TBSPs olive oil
- 2TBSPs rosemary, chopped
- ½ tsp cumin
- Half tsp nutmeg

- 120ml sour cream
- Salt and black pepper to the taste

Procedure step by step:
1. Combine the pork, artichokes, and other ingredients in a pan that will fit in your air fryer. Prepare at 200 degrees Celsius for 25 minutes.
2. It is important to divide up the food in the bowls..

Dietary composition:
Calories 413, Fat 29, Fiber 4, Carbs 10, Protein 28

82. Mustard Lamb Loin Chops

Preparing time: 15 minutes
Time needed to cook: 30 minutes
Number of portions: 4

Required Material:
- 8 (each 113g) lamb loin chops
- 2 TBSPs Dijon mustard
- 1 TBSP fresh lemon juice
- ½ tsp olive oil
- 1 tsp dried tarragon
- Salt and black pepper, to taste

Procedure step by step:
1. Grease the basket and raise the Air Fryer's temperature to 200 degrees Celsius
2. In a large bowl, combine the olive oil, tarragon, salt, pepper, lemon juice, and mustard.
3. After brushing the chops with the mustard sauce, place them in the Air fryer.
4. Serve while still hot after cooking for approximately 15 minutes with one flip.

Dietary composition:
Calories: 322, Fat: 20g, Carbohydrates: 2g, Sugar: 0g, Protein: 32g, Sodium: 268mg

83. Simple Beef Burgers

Preparing time: 20 minutes
Time needed to cook: 12 minutes
Number of portions: 6

Required Material:
- 907g of ground beef
- 12 cheddar cheese slices
- 12 dinner rolls
- 6 TBSPs tomato ketchup
- Salt and black pepper, to taste

Procedure step by step:
1. Grease the basket and preheat the Air fryer to 200 degrees Celsius.
2. In a bowl, combine a wide range of spices with the meat.
3. Form the beef mixture into uniform mini-patties, then place half of them in the air fryer's cooking basket.
4. Put a piece of cheese on top of the burgers and cook them for around fifteen minutes.
5. Distribute some ketchup on each roll after adding a patty to the center.
6. Complete the remaining batch immediately and serve.

Dietary composition:
Calories: 577, Fat: 33g, Carbohydrates: 30g, Sugar: 5g, Protein: 37g, Sodium: 685mg

84. Nutmeg Beef Mix

Preparing time: 10 minutes
Time needed to cook: 30 minutes
Number of portions: 4

Required Material:
- 907g beef stew meat, cubed
- 1tsp nutmeg, ground
- 2TBSPs avocado oil
- ½ tsp chili powder
- 60ml beef stock
- 2TBSPs chives, chopped

- Salt and black pepper to the taste

Procedure step by step:
1. Cook the pork, nutmeg, and other ingredients for 30 minutes at 200 degrees Celsius in a dish that will fit in your air fryer.
2. Divide the ingredients into individual servings and serve.

Dietary composition:
Calories 405, Fat 23, Fiber 0, Carbs 2, Protein 40g

85. Herbed Pork Burgers

Preparing time: 15 minutes
Time needed to cook: 45 minutes
Number of portions: 8

Required Material:
- 2 small onions, chopped
- 595g ground pork
- 2 tsps fresh basil, chopped
- 8 burger buns
- 120g cheddar cheese, grated
- 2 tsps mustard
- 2 tsps garlic puree
- 2 tsps ml tomato puree
- Salt and freshly ground black pepper, to taste
- 2 tsps dried mixed herbs, crushed

Procedure step by step:
1. The recommended temperature for an air fryer is 200 degrees Celsius, and the equipment should be used with an oiled basket.
2. Leave aside the cheese and the bread and add everything else to the casserole.
3. Make 8 patties from the pork mixture and place them in the air fryer's frying basket. Bake for 45 minutes and flip them once.
4. Once ready, compose burgers bread using patties and cheese and serve.

Dietary composition:
Calories: 428, Fat: 28g, Carbohydrates: 20g, Sugar:

4g, Protein: 24g, Sodium: 543mg

86. Chinese Style Pork Meatballs

Preparing time: 15 minutes
Time needed to cook: 20 minutes
Number of portions: 3

Required Material:
- 1 egg, beaten
- 170g ground pork
- 30g cornstarch
- 1 tsp oyster sauce
- ½ TBSP light soy sauce
- ½ tsp sesame oil
- ¼ tsp five-spice powder
- ½ TBSP olive oil
- ¼ tsp brown sugar

Procedure step by step:
1. Prepare the basket greasing it and the Air fryer preheated to 200 degrees Celsius.
2. Except for the cornstarch and oil, combine all of the ingredients in a bowl and mix until smooth.
3. Roll the dough into balls and pass them into a bowl with cornstarch.
4. The meatballs may be produced and served warm in less than ten minutes after being coated in the cornstarch solution and then transferred to the basket of an Air fryer.

Dietary composition:
Calories: 210, Fat: 14g, Carbohydrates: 9g, Sugar: 1g, Protein: 13g, Sodium: 463mg

87. Veggie Stuffed Beef Rolls

Preparing time: 20 minutes
Time needed to cook: 14 minutes
Number of portions: 6

Required Material:
- 2 pounds beef flank steak, pounded to 1/8-inch thickness

- 6 Provolone cheese slices
- 85 g roasted red bell peppers
- 175 ml fresh baby spinach
- 3 TBSPs prepared pesto
- Salt and black pepper, to taste

Procedure step by step:
1. Take a basket of your air fryer. To warm the Air fryer set at 200° Celsius.
2. Put some pesto on a plate and arrange the meat on top.
3. Spinach and red peppers should be sprinkled with cheese and placed on top.
4. Use toothpicks to secure the steak once you have wrapped it tightly around the filling.
5. For 14 minutes at 200 degrees Celsius, flipping the basket once, the roll will be perfectly cooked.
6. Serve directly.

Dietary composition:
Calories: 409, Fat: 24.2g, Carbohydrates: 3.8g, Protein: 42.5g, Sodium: 507mg, Fiber: 0.7g

88. Lamb and Mustard Sauce

Preparing time: 10 minutes
Time needed to cook: 25 minutes
Number of portions: 4

Required Material:
- 908 g lamb chops
- 2TBSPs mustard
- 2TBSPs butter, melted
- 235 ml beef stock
- 1tsp coriander, ground
- 1tsp sweet paprika
- Salt and black pepper to the taste

Procedure step by step:
1. Toss the lamb chops with the mustard and the other spices in the pan before frying for 25 minutes at 200 degrees C in an air fryer.
2. Individual portions of the mixture are

recommended.

Dietary composition:
Calories: 562, Fat: 41.6g, Carbohydrates: 3.3g, Protein: 43.3g, Sodium: 582mg, Fiber: 0.6g

89. Beef with Apples and Plums

Preparing time: 10 minutes
Time needed to cook: 30 minutes
Number of portions: 4

Required Material:
- 908 g beef stew meat, cubed
- 235 ml apples, cored and cubed
- 235 ml plums, pitted and halved
- 2TBSPs butter, melted
- Salt and black pepper to the taste
- 120 ml red wine
- 1TBSP chives, chopped

Procedure step by step:
1. Putting the meat, apples, and the other ingredients in the air fryer pan, they cook for thirty minutes at a temperature of 198 degrees Celsius.
2. Afterward, the food is uniformly distributed among the serving plates, and it is served immediately.

Dietary composition:
Calories: 409, Fat: 19.5g, Carbohydrates: 8.6g, Protein: 40.9g, Sodium: 226mg, Fiber: 1.7g

90. Tomato Stuffed Pork Roll

Preparing time: 20 minutes
Time needed to cook: 15 minutes
Number of portions: 4

Required Material:
- 1 scallion, chopped
- 59 ml sun-dried tomatoes, chopped finely
- 2 TBSPs fresh parsley, chopped
- 4 (170 g) pork cutlets, pounded slightly
- Salt and freshly ground black pepper, to

taste
- 2 tsps paprika
- ½ TBSP olive oil

Procedure step by step:
1. Air fryer basket should be greased and device heated to 200 degrees C
2. Scallions, tomatoes, parsley, salt, and pepper should all be combined in a bowl.
3. Each cutlet should be topped with tomato filling, rolled up, and held together with a cocktail stick.
4. Oil the rolls, then season them with salt & pepper and paprika.
5. Rolls should be cooked for 15 minutes in a preheated Air fryer, flipping only one time.
6. Affix to a hot dish and savor.

Dietary composition:
Calories: 291, Fat: 14g, Carbohydrates: 3g, Protein: 38g, Sodium: 190mg, Fiber: 1g

91. Lamb Meatballs

Preparing time: 22 minutes
Number of portions: 8

Required Material:
- 113 g. lamb meat; minced
- 1 tbsp. oregano; chopped.
- 1/2 tbsp. lemon zest
- 1 egg; whisked
- Cooking spray
- Salt and black pepper to taste

Procedure step by step:
1. Put all the ingredients (excluding the cooking spray) into a bowl and mix well.
2. Form the meat into walnut-sized balls by rolling it in your hands.
3. Cook the meatballs for 15 minutes at 200 degrees Celsius after spraying them with frying spray and placing them in the air fryer's cooking basket. Serve by dividing among separate plates.

Dietary composition:
Calories: 47, Fat: 3g, Protein: 4g, Carbohydrates: 1g, Sodium: 73mg

92. Delicious Sausage

Preparing time: 25 minutes
Number of portions: 4

Required Material:
- 6 pork sausage links; halved
- 1 red onion; sliced
- 1 tbsp. olive oil
- 1 tbsp. rosemary; chopped.
- 2 garlic cloves; minced
- 1 tbsp. sweet paprika
- Salt and black pepper to taste

Procedure step by step:
1. Put everything together in a pan that can go into an air fryer.
2. Cooking for 20 minutes at a temperature of 182 degrees Celsius will cause the sauce to boil. Serve by dividing among separate bowls.

Dietary composition:
Calories: 326, Fat: 26.5g, Carbohydrates: 6.8g, Protein: 15.3g, Fiber: 1.6g

93. Beef, Arugula and Leeks

Preparing time: 22 minutes
Number of portions: 4

Required Material:
- 450 g. ground beef
- 140 g baby arugula
- 1 tbsp. olive oil
- 2 tbsp. tomato paste
- 3 leeks; roughly chopped.
- Salt and black pepper to taste

Procedure step by step:
1. Mix the meat, leeks, salt, pepper, oil, and tomato paste in an air fryer-safe pan.
2. The recommended cooking time is 12

minutes at 190 degrees Celsius.

3. Mix in the arugula just before serving. Dish out.

Dietary composition:
Calories: 292, Fat: 20g, Protein: 24g, Carbohydrates: 7g, Fiber: 2g, Sugar: 3g, Sodium: 402mg

94. BBQ Pork Ribs

Number of portions: 4
Preparing time: 15 minutes
Time needed to cook: 26 minutes

Ingredients
- 59 ml honey, divided
- 177 ml BBQ sauce
- 2 TBSPs tomato ketchup
- 1 TBSP Worcestershire sauce*
- 1 TBSP soy sauce
- ½ tsp garlic powder
- Freshly ground white pepper, to taste
- 794g pork ribs

Procedure step by step:
1. Combine everything on the plate except the pork ribs and stir in the 45 mL of honey.
2. Put the pork ribs in the pan and cover them well in the sauce.
3. The suggested marinating period in the fridge is 20 minutes.
4. Put the air fryer on a setting of 180 degrees Celsius. Butter up a basket for the air fryer.
5. Spread the ribs out in a single layer in the air fryer basket.
6. You should air fry each side for around 13 minutes.
7. Take the ribs out of the air fryer and serve them on plates.
8. Serve immediately with the remaining honey drizzled over top.

Dietary composition:
Calories: 584, Fat: 39g, Carbohydrates: 26g,

Protein: 31g, Sugar: 23g, Sodium: 842mg
(Note - Worcestershire sauce* - The other ingredients that make up this savory sauce usually include onions, molasses, high fructose corn syrup: depending on the country of production), salt, garlic, tamarind, cloves, chili pepper extract, water, and natural flavorings.

95. Marinated Lamb and Veggies

Preparing time: 40 Minutes
Number of portions: 4

Required Material:
- 1 carrot; chopped
- 1 onion; sliced
- 1/2 tbsp. olive oil
- 225 g lamb loin; sliced
- 85 g bean sprouts
- For the marinade:
- 1 garlic clove; minced
- 1/2 apple; grated
- 2 tbsp. orange juice
- 5 tbsp. soy sauce
- 1 tbsp. sugar
- 1 tbsp. ginger; grated
- 1 small yellow onion; grated
- Salt and black pepper to the taste

Procedure step by step:
1. Combine a shredded onion, an apple, a tbsp ginger, a tbsp garlic, a cup orange juice, a cup sugar, a tsp of black pepper, and a pound lamb in a bowl, and leave to marinate.
2. To make this dish, heat the olive oil in a skillet that can go in your air fryer over medium heat, then add the chopped onion, carrot, and bean sprouts.
3. To prepare the marinated lamb, place the pan in an air fryer warmed to 182 degrees Celsius for 25 minutes. Dish it out and serve.

Dietary composition:
Calories: 313kcal, Fat: 13g, Saturated Fat: 4g,

Cholesterol: 74mg, Sodium: 1836mg, Potassium: 566mg, Carbohydrates: 20g, Fiber: 2g, Sugar: 13g, Protein: 28g

96. Flank Steak Beef

Preparing time: 10 minutes
Time needed to cook: 20 minutes
Number of portions: 4

Required Material:

- 454 g flank steaks, sliced
- 28 g xanthum gum
- 2 tsp vegetable oil
- ½ tsp ginger
- 120 ml soy sauce
- 1 TBSP garlic, minced
- 120 ml water
- 180 g swerve, packed

Procedure step by step:

1. Set the Air fryer temperature to 198 degrees Celsius and oil the basket.
2. Then, place the steaks in the Air fryer basket and coat both sides with xantham gum.
3. After 10 minutes in the oven, plate it in a serving dish.
4. In a separate pot, simmer the other sauce ingredients while you wait.
5. Serve after combining the sauce with the steaks.

Dietary composition:

Calories: 398, Total fat: 21g, Saturated fat: 8g, Cholesterol: 102mg, Sodium: 2019mg, Total carbohydrate: 10g, Dietary fiber: 1g, Protein: 40g

97. Crispy Potatoes and Parsley

Preparing time: 10 minutes
Time needed to cook: 10 minutes
Number of portions:4

Required Material:

- 494g gold potatoes, cut into wedges
- Salt and black pepper to the taste
- 2 TBSPs olive
- 15ml Juice from ½ lemon
- 15g parsley leaves, chopped

Procedure step by step:

1. Sprinkle potatoes with a mixture of pepper and spices, then drizzle with lemon juice and olive oil and fry after inserting in an air fryer at 175 degrees Celsius for 10 minutes.
2. After plating, sprinkle with parsley.

Dietary composition:
Calories: 41; Fat: 1.3g; Fiber: 0.5g; Carbs: 6g; Protein: 2g

98. Indian Turnips Salad

Preparing time: 10 minutes
Time needed to cook: 12 minutes
Number of portions:4

Required Material:

- 567g of turnips, peeled and chopped
- 1 tsp garlic, minced
- 1 tsp ginger, grated
- 2 yellow onions, chopped
- 2 tomatoes, chopped
- 1 tsp cumin, ground
- 1 tsp coriander, ground

- 2 green chilies, chopped
- ½ tsp turmeric powder
- 2 TBSPs butter
- Salt and black pepper to the taste
- A handful of coriander leaves, chopped

Procedure step by step:

1. First, loose the butter in a skillet that will fit in your air fryer, then add the green chilies, garlic, and ginger and cook for 1 minute, stirring often.
2. Cook turnips in an air fryer for 10 minutes at 175 °C after adding other components, and a few other spices.
3. Sprinkle each serving with fresh coriander, and serve.

Dietary composition:
Calories: 141; Fat: 8g; Fiber: 6g; Carbs: 14g; Protein: 2g

99. Artichoke Spinach Casserole

Preparing time: 30 minutes
Number of portions: 4

Required Material:

- 79.5g full-fat mayonnaise
- 227g full-fat cream cheese; softened.
- 40g diced yellow onion
- 79.5ml full-fat sour cream.
- 40g chopped pickled jalapeños.
- 120g fresh spinach; chopped
- 230g cauliflower florets; chopped
- 190g artichoke hearts; chopped
- 1 tbsp. salted butter; melted.

Procedure step by step:

1. Mix the butter, onion, cream cheese, mayonnaise, and sour cream in a large basin. Combine the artichokes, cauliflower, spinach, and jalapenos.
2. Then, fill a 4-cup capacity circular baking dish with the mixture. Wrap in foil, then put in the air fryer.
3. Fix the timer for 15 seconds and adjust

the temperature to 187 degrees. Take the foil off in the last 2 minutes of cooking to get a nice browning on top. Warmly serve.

Dietary composition:
Calories: 447; Protein: 9g; Fiber: 4g; Fat: 42g; Carbs: 11g

100. Cheese Zucchini Boats

Preparing time: 35 minutes
Number of portions: 2

Required Material:

- 2 medium zucchini
- 60g full-fat ricotta cheese
- 28g shredded mozzarella cheese
- 60g low-carb, no-sugar-added pasta sauce.
- 2 tbsp. grated vegetarian Parmesan cheese
- 1 tbsp. avocado oil
- ¼ tsp. garlic powder.
- ½ tsp. dried parsley.
- ¼ tsp. dried oregano.

Procedure step by step:

1. To prepare the zucchini boats, eliminate the top and bottom, cut them in half (lengthwise), and use a spoon to remove some of the pulp from the center. Fill each shell with oil and sauce.
2. Create a filling with ricotta, mozzarella, oregano, garlic powder, and chopped parsley in a medium basin. Then, divide among the zucchini boats.
3. Insert the air fryer basket with the filled zucchini boats and the heat up to 175 degrees Celsius; set the timer for 20 minutes.
4. Carefully remove the food from the frying basket by using tongs or a spatula.
5. Sprinkle some grated Parmesan cheese on top before serving.

Dietary composition:
Calories: 223; Protein: 12g; Fiber: 3g; Fat: 16g; Carbs: 9g

101.   Spaghetti Squash Alfredo

Preparing time: 25 minutes
Number of portions: 2

Required Material:

- 227g cooked spaghetti squash
- 28g grated vegetarian Parmesan cheese.
- 57g shredded Italian blend cheese
- 118ml low-carb Alfredo sauce
- 2 tbsp. salted butter; melted.
- ¼ tsp. ground peppercorn
- ½ tsp. garlic powder.
- 1 tsp. dried parsley.

Procedure step by step:

1. Use a fork to pull the spaghetti squash strings out of the shell. Add it with butter, and Alfredo sauce to a big bowl. Put Parmesan, garlic powder, chopped parsley, and peppercorns on top.
2. Place into a round baking dish with a 4-cup capacity and sprinkle with shredded cheese. Put the dish into the basket of the air fryer. Set the setting to 160°C and set the timer for 15 minutes.
3. When the cheese is done, it will be brown and melting. Serve straight away.

Dietary composition:

Calories: 382; Protein: 13g; Fiber: 3g; Fat: 31g; Carbs: 15g

102.   Classic ratatouille

Preparing time: 30 minutes
Number of portions: 2

Ingredients

- 1 tbsp olive oil
- 3 roma tomatoes, thinly sliced
- 2 garlic cloves, minced
- 1 zucchini, thinly sliced
- 2 yellow bell peppers, sliced
- 1 tbsp vinegar

- 2 tbsp herbs de Provence
- Salt and black pepper to taste

Directions

1. Set the air fryer to 200 degrees C and put all of the items in a bowl.
2. Add salt and pepper, then stir the vegetables until they are well covered.
3. Put the vegetables in a round baking dish and put it in the oven. Cook for 15 minutes while shaking the pan every so often.
4. After the timer goes off, let it sit for 5 more minutes.

Dietary composition:

Calories: 110, Protein: 3g, Fat: 6g, Carbs: 14g

103.   Vegetable spring rolls

Preparing time: 15 minutes
Number of portions: 4

Ingredients

- ½ cabbage, grated
- 2 carrots, grated
- 1 tsp minced ginger
- 1 tsp minced garlic
- 1 tsp sesame oil
- 1 tsp soy sauce
- 1 tsp sesame seeds
- ½ tsp salt
- 1 tsp olive oil
- 1 package of spring roll wrappers

Directions

1. First, throw everything into one big dish.
2. Then, put the stuffed spring rolls in a single layer on a baking sheet and repeat with the other ingredients.
3. Bake at 187 degrees C for 5 minutes.

Dietary composition:

Calories: 107, Protein: 2,4g, Fat: 3,6g, Carbs: 17,6g

104.   Herbed Carrots

Number of portions: 8
Preparing time: 15 minutes
Time needed to cook: 14 minutes

Ingredients

- 6 large carrots, peeled and sliced lengthwise
- 2 TBSPs olive oil
- ½ TBSP fresh oregano, chopped
- ½ TBSP fresh parsley, chopped
- Salt and ground black pepper, as required

Procedure step by step:

1. Air fryer to 182 °C and fryer basket should be greased.
2. Mix carrot slices and oil in a bowl. Layer carrot slices in the air fryer basket.
3. Fry twelve minutes. Take away from the air fryer and evenly dust the carrots with herbs, and spices.
4. Fry again for 2 more minutes.
5. Take away carrot slices from fryer and place on plates.

Dietary composition:

Calories: 55, Carbohydrate: 5g, Protein: 1g, Fat: 4g, Sugar: 2g, Sodium: 55mg

105.   Spices Stuffed Eggplants

Preparing time: 15 minutes
Time needed to cook: 12 minutes
Number of portions: 4

Required Material:

- 8 baby eggplants
- 4 tsps olive oil, divided
- ¾ TBSP dry mango powder
- ¾ TBSP ground coriander
- ½ tsp ground cumin
- ½ tsp ground turmeric
- ½ tsp garlic powder
- Salt, to taste

Procedure step by step:

1. First, lubricate an Air fryer basket and preheat the Air fryer to 187 degrees C.
2. Cut two slits, stem side up, into the bottom of each eggplant, then need to stuff each eggplant with a mixture of one tsp of oil and spices.
3. Brush the leftover oil on the eggplants' exteriors and lay them in the Air fryer basket. Bake for 12 minutes, then serve hot on a platter.

Dietary composition:

Calories: 95, Fats: 6g, Carbohydrates: 10g, Sugar: 4g, Proteins: 2g, Sodium: 50mg

106.   Curried Eggplant

Number of portions: 2
Preparing time: 15 minutes
Time needed to cook: 10 minutes

Ingredients

- 1 large eggplant, cut into ½-inch thick slices
- 1 garlic clove, minced
- ½ fresh red chili, chopped
- 1 TBSP vegetable oil
- ¼ tsp curry powder
- Salt, as required

Procedure step by step:

1. Air fryer's setting to 150 degrees C. Grease up a basket for an air fryer.
2. Put all the ingredients in a bowl and mix them well.
3. Arrange the eggplant pieces in a single layer in the air fryer basket.
4. Cook for about 10 minutes in the air fryer, shaking once about halfway through.
5. Take the eggplant slices out of the air fryer and put them on plates.

Dietary composition:

Calories: 110, Carbohydrate: 11g, Protein: 2g, Fat: 7g, Sugar: 5g, Sodium: 130mg

107. Green Beans and Lime Sauce

Preparing time: 13 minutes
Number of portions: 4

Required Material:

- 454 g green beans, trimmed
- 2 tbsp. ghee; melted
- 1 tbsp. lime juice
- 1 tsp. chili powder
- A pinch of salt and black pepper

Procedure step by step:

1. For the first step, whisk together the ghee and everything else in the bowl, except the green beans. Now, incorporate the green beans in the lime sauce.
2. Then, for 8 minutes at 200 degrees Celsius, place them in the basket of your air fryer. Rapidly serve.

Dietary composition:
Calories: 97, Fat: 8.3g, Carbohydrates: 6.1g, Fiber: 2.7g, Protein: 1.8g, Sugar: 2.2g

108. Roasted Veggie Bowl

Preparing time: 25 minutes
Number of portions: 2

Required Material:

- ¼ medium white onion; peeled.and sliced ¼-inch thick
- ½ medium green bell pepper; seeded and sliced ¼-inch thick
- 240 ml broccoli florets
- 240 ml quartered Brussels sprouts
- 120 ml cauliflower florets
- 1 tbsp. coconut oil
- ½ tsp. garlic powder.
- ½ tsp. cumin
- 2 tsp. chili powder

Procedure step by step:

1. In a large bowl, combine all of the ingredients and toss to coat the veggies. Fill the air fryer's basket with vegetables.
2. Then, set the timer for 15 minutes and the temperature to 182 degrees Celsius. Shake the pan two or three times while it cooks. Warmly serve.

Dietary composition:
Calories: 137, Fat: 9g, Carbohydrates: 14g, Fiber: 5g, Protein: 4g, Sugar: 5g

109. Peanut Butter Cookies

Preparing time: 13 minutes
Number of portions: 8

Required Material:

- 1 large egg.
- 80 g granular erythritol.
- 240 ml no-sugar-added smooth peanut butter.
- 1 tsp. vanilla extract.

Procedure step by step:

1. Using a sizable bowl, thoroughly combine all of the ingredients. After 2 more minutes of stirring, the liquid should have begun to thicken.
2. Form the dough into eight balls, then carefully flatten them into disks.
3. Line the basket of your air fryer with adequate paper that you have cut to size. As needed, work in batches the cookies.
4. Adjust the timer for 8 minutes and the temperature to 160 degrees Celsius.
5. At the 6-minute mark, give the cookies a flip. When fully chilled, serve.

Dietary composition:
Calories: 191, Fat: 16g, Carbohydrates: 6g, Fiber: 2g, Protein: 8g, Sugar: 1g

110. Sesame Seeds Bok Choy

Preparing time: 10 minutes
Time needed to cook: 6 minutes
Number of portions: 4

Required Material:

- 4 bunches baby bok choy, bottoms removed and leaves separated
- 1 tsp sesame seeds
- Olive oil cooking spray
- 1 tsp garlic powder

Procedure step by step:

1. Grease the Air fryer basket. Air-fryer at 320° Celsius.
2. Then, spray the bok choy leaves with cooking spray and arrange them in the Air fryer basket.
3. After shaking the pan twice, sprinkle with garlic powder and proceed for another 6 minutes.
4. Serve the bok choy in individual servings, sprinkled with toasted sesame seeds.

Dietary composition:

Calories: 26, Fat: 0.7g, Carbohydrates: 4g, Sugar: 1.9g, Protein: 2.5g, Sodium: 98mg

111.　Salsa Stuffed Eggplants

Number of portions: 2
Preparing time: 15 minutes
Time needed to cook: 25 minutes

Ingredients

- 1 large eggplant
- 2 tsps olive oil, divided
- 2 tsps fresh lemon juice, divided
- 8 cherry tomatoes, quartered
- 2 TBSPs tomato salsa
- ½ TBSP fresh parsley
- Salt and ground black pepper, as required

Procedure step by step:

1. Set temperature at 200°C. Air fryer basket grease.
2. Put eggplant in air fryer basket, then fry 15 mins.
3. After air-frying cut eggplant in half and brush using one tsp of oil.

4. Pass the air fryer to 180°C and place again cut-side-up eggplant for another 10 minutes.
5. Carefully scoop out the pulp, and drizzle eggplant with lemon juice.
6. Put eggplant in a bowl. Mix tomatoes, salsa, parsley, salt, black pepper, remaining oil, and lemon juice.
7. Serve salsa-stuffed eggplant.

Dietary composition:

Calories: 152kcal, Fat: 10g, Saturated Fat: 1g, Carbohydrates: 14g, Fiber: 8g, Sugar: 9g, Protein: 4g, Sodium: 320mg

112.　Basil Tomatoes

Number of portions: 2
Preparing time: 10 minutes
Time needed to cook: 10 minutes

Ingredients

- 2 tomatoes, halved
- Olive oil cooking spray
- Salt and ground black pepper, as required
- 1 TBSP fresh basil, chopped

Procedure step by step:

1. Get your air fryer up to a temperature of 160 degrees Celsius. Butter up a basket for the air fryer.
2. After cutting the tomatoes in half lengthwise, spray each half with cooking spray and season with salt, black pepper, and basil.
3. Place the tomato halves, cut-side up, in the air fryer basket. Cook for about 10 minutes until done.
4. Take the tomatoes out of the air fryer and place them on individual plates. Serve hot.

Dietary composition:

Calories: 30kcal, Fat: 1g, Sodium: 100mg, Potassium: 300mg, Carbohydrates: 5g, Fiber: 2g, Sugar: 3g, Protein: 1g

113. Carrot Peanut Butter Soup

Preparing time: 5 minutes
Time needed to cook: 15 minutes
Number of portions: 4

Required Material:

- 8 carrots, peeled and chopped
- 1 onion, chopped
- 3 garlic cloves, peeled
- 414ml coconut milk
- 355ml chicken stock
- 64g peanut butter
- 1 tbsp. curry paste
- Pepper
- Salt

Procedure step by step:

1. Put everything in the air fryer except the salt and pepper and stir well.
2. Cover the pot with a lid and cook for 15 minutes.
3. Use a stick mixer to puree the soup until it is smooth.
4. Add pepper and salt to the soup. Serve and enjoy.

Dietary composition:

Calories: 240, Fat: 18 g, Sodium: 590 mg, Carbohydrates: 18 g, Fiber: 4 g, Sugar: 9 g, Protein: 7 g.

114.   Air fryer Golden Lentil and Spinach Soup

Preparing time: 10 minutes
Time needed to cook: 25 minutes
Number of portions: 4

Required Material:

- 2 tsps of olive oil
- 1/2 yellow onion, diced
- 2 carrots, peeled and diced
- 1 celery stalk, diced
- 4 garlic cloves, minced
- 2 tsps ground cumin
- 1 tsp ground turmeric
- 1 tsp dried thyme
- 1 tsp kosher salt
- ¼ tsp ground black pepper
- 200g dry brown lentils, rinsed well
- 946ml low-sodium vegetable broth
- 227g of baby spinach

Procedure step by step:

1. First, put some oil in the air fryer and choose the saute setting. Once the pan is heated, toss in some chopped vegetables. For approximately 5 minutes while tossing periodically, saute until tender.
2. Put in some salt, pepper, thyme, cumin, turmeric, garlic, and onion. Stir for a minute while the food cooks. Add the lentils and broth and mix well.
3. Set the timer for 12 minutes and click the button. At the end Add the spinach and season with salt and pepper.

Dietary composition:
Calories: 241, Fat: 5.8g, Sodium: 571mg, Carbohydrates: 36.8g, Fiber: 16.4g, Sugar: 6.2g, Protein: 14.1g.

115.   Spicy Mushroom Soup

Preparing time: 5 minutes
Time needed to cook: 11 minutes
Number of portions: 2

Required Material:

- 70g mushrooms, chopped
- ½ tsp. chili powder
- 2 tsp. garam masala
- 3 tbsp. olive oil
- 1 tsp. fresh lemon juice
- 1.18lt chicken stock
- 20g fresh celery, chopped
- 2 garlic cloves, crushed
- 1 onion, chopped
- ½ tsp. black pepper
- 1 tsp sea salt

Procedure step by step:

1. First, add oil to the air fryer, and then turn it to the Sauté setting.
2. Just add garlic and onions to the mix and you will be good to go. Saute for 5 minutes.
3. To amp up the heat, sprinkle in additional cayenne pepper and garam masala. Maintain a steady temperature for a full minute. While stirring, add the remaining ingredients.
4. Cover and cook on manual high pressure for five minutes.
5. Immediately after quickly releasing some of the pressure, the lid can be taken off.
6. The soup should be blended until smooth before serving.

Dietary composition:
Calories: 251, Fat: 21g, Sodium: 1545mg, Carbohydrates: 11g, Fiber: 2g, Sugar: 4g, Protein: 6g.

116.   Creamy Squash Soup

Preparing time: 5 minutes
Time needed to cook: 15 minutes
Number of portions: 4

Required Material:

- 1814g butternut squash, peeled, seeded, and cubed
- 946ml beef stock

- ½ tsp. sage
- 1 tsp. thyme
- 2 garlic cloves, minced
- 1 onion, chopped
- 2 tbsp olive oil
- Pepper
- Salt

Procedure step by step:

1. First, add oil to the air fryer, and then turn it to the Sauté setting.
2. Just add garlic and onions to the mix and you will be good to go. Saute for 5 minutes.
3. Season the final dish with salt, pepper, sage, and thyme. Alter the status quo for a while.
4. Place the squash and stock in a pot and bring to a simmer. Good blending.
5. Cook the food in a pressure cooker for 10 minutes at high pressure on the manual setting, covered.
6. Immediately after quickly releasing some of the pressure, the lid can be taken off.
7. If you use an immersion blender to purée the soup, you may make it silky and smooth. Give and take pleasure.

Dietary composition:
Calories: 239, Total fat: 7g, Sodium: 488mg, Total carbohydrate: 43g, Fiber: 8g, Sugars: 9g, Protein: 6g.

117.   Kale Beef Soup

Preparing time: 15 minutes
Time needed to cook: 43 minutes
Number of portions: 4

Required Material:

- 454g beef stew meat
- 1 tsp. cayenne pepper
- 3 garlic cloves, crushed
- 946ml chicken broth
- 30ml olive oil
- 100g kale, chopped

- 1 onion, sliced
- ¼ tsp. black pepper
- ½ tsp. salt

Procedure step by step:

1. Pour oil into the air fryer, and then select the Sauté preset.
2. Garlic and scallions should be used to prepare soup. Continue cooking for three minutes longer.
3. Cook the meat for five minutes in a skillet.
4. The recommended seasonings for the chowder are cayenne pepper, black pepper, and salt. Blend well.
5. Cover and cook under manual high pressure for a total of 25 minutes.
6. After swiftly releasing a portion of the container's internal pressure, remove the lid.
7. Include kale and blend it into the mixture. Ten minutes should be spent doing nothing.
8. Combine all ingredients, then serve.

Dietary composition:
Calories: 272, Fat: 14g, Carbohydrates: 7g, Fiber: 1g, Protein: 28g, Sodium: 980mg

118.   Creamy Cauliflower Soup

Preparing time: 10 minutes
Time needed to cook: 32 minutes
Number of portions: 4

Required Material:

- 300g cauliflower florets
- 1 tsp. pumpkin pie spice
- 1.175ml chicken broth
- 3 tbsp. olive oil
- 1 onion, chopped
- ¼ tsp. salt

Procedure step by step:

1. Put some oil in the air fryer, and then set it to Sauté.

2. In a pot, heat the oil over medium heat and cook the onion for five minutes.

3. After one minute, you should add cauliflower and cook it. Put in some stock and season it with salt. Cook for a total of 24 minutes with the lid on, the pot closed, and the pressure cooker set to manual high pressure.

4. After letting some of the air out quickly, take the lid off.

5. Use a stick mixer to get the soup as smooth as possible.

6. Mix in the pumpkin pie spice mix. For two minutes, you should use the sauté setting.

7. Offer and enjoy.

Dietary composition:
Calories: 120, Fat: 9g, Carbohydrates: 7g, Fiber: 2g, Sugar: 3g, Protein: 3g, Sodium: 800mg

119.   Air fryer Angel Hair Soup

Preparing time: 5 minutes
Time needed to cook: 15 minutes
Number of portions: 4

Required Material:
- 946ml of low-sodium chicken broth
- 3 Tbsp of tomato sauce
- 226g of angel hair pasta
- 7 leaves of fresh basil
- 2 tbsp of olive oil
- 60g of parmesan cheese to serve
- 2 Peeled and diced carrots
- 1 Peeled and cubed potato
- 60ml of chickpeas

Procedure step by step:
1. Place the chickpeas, carrots, tomato sauce, basil, oil, and broth into the air fryer.
2. Using the sauté button, cook the items quickly for about 5 minutes.
3. After adding chicken stock, put the Air fryer's lid back on.

4. Keep the pressure at the highest level possible for about ten minutes.

5. When the timer goes off, take the lid off the pot and add the angel hair pasta right away.

6. Put everything in the pot, turn up the heat to high, and let it boil for five minutes.

7. Once the basil has been added, cook for one more minute.

8. Arrange in a bowl and top with chopped Parmesan cheese and tortilla chips. Offer and enjoy!

Dietary composition:
Calories: 268, Fat: 8g, Cholesterol: 4mg, Sodium: 414mg, Carbohydrates: 41g, Fiber: 4g, Sugar: 4g, Protein: 9g.

120.   Simple Kale Chicken Soup

Preparing time: 5 minutes
Time needed to cook: 15 minutes
Number of portions: 4

Required Material:
- 450g chicken breast, cooked and chopped
- 2 tsp. garlic, minced
- ½ tsp. cinnamon
- 946ml vegetable broth
- 1 onion, diced
- 340g kale
- 1 tsp. salt

Procedure step by step:
1. The ingredients should be placed in the air fryer and mixed together before cooking.
2. Cover and cook on manual high pressure for five minutes. After a ten-minute natural release, follow with the rapid-release instructions.
3. Mix, then serve on a sizzling plate.

Dietary composition:
Calories: 174, Fat: 4g, Cholesterol: 60mg, Sodium: 1200mg, Carbohydrates: 12g, Fiber: 3g, Sugar: 3g, Protein: 24g.

121.   Coconut Chicken Soup

Preparing time: 5 minutes
Time needed to cook: 15 minutes
Number of portions: 4

Required Material:

- 453.6g chicken thighs, boneless and cut into chunks
- 475ml Swiss chard, chopped
- 150g celery stalks, chopped
- 1 tsp. turmeric
- 1 tbsp. chicken broth base
- 283.5g can of tomato
- 237ml coconut milk
- 1 tbsp. ginger, grated
- 4 garlic cloves, minced
- 1 onion, chopped

Procedure step by step:

1. A 120ml of coconut milk, broth base, a TBSP of turmeric, tomatoes, ginger, garlic, and a shallot should be blended together in a blender. Avoid lumps by mixing well.
2. Add the chicken, Swiss chard, and celery to the air fryer and stir everything together. Good blending.
3. Cover and cook on manual high pressure for five minutes.
4. The instructions for the expedited release come after a ten-minute period of natural release.
5. Combine everything well after adding the remaining coconut oil.
6. Serve and savor.

Dietary composition:
Calories: 335, Total Fat: 20g, Cholesterol: 94mg, Sodium: 361mg, Total Carbohydrates: 14g, Fiber: 3g, Sugars: 6g, Protein: 27g.

122.   Taco Cheese Soup

Preparing time: 10 minutes
Time needed to cook: 25 minutes
Number of portions: 8

Required Material:

- 454g ground beef
- 454g ground pork
- 56g Monterey Jack cheese, grated
- 2 tbsp. parsley, chopped
- 946ml beef broth
- 567g. can tomatoes
- 454g. cream cheese
- 2 tbsp. taco seasonings

Procedure step by step:

1. Alternate between the two types of ground beef and cook them in the air fryer for 10 minutes at high heat.
2. Put in some taco seasoning, some tomato sauce, and some cream cheese. Throw everything into the bowl and mix well.
3. Remove the lid after quickly releasing part of the pressure from the container after cooking for fifteen minutes at manual high pressure.
4. Ignore the naysayers and know that there is a method to my madness. Add some grated cheese and enjoy.

Dietary composition:
Calories: 492, Fat: 37g, Cholesterol: 147mg, Sodium: 1235mg, Carbohydrates: 8g, Fiber: 2g, Sugar: 4g, Protein: 32g.

123.   Air fryer Italian Beef Stew

Preparing time: 10 minutes
Time needed to cook: 35 minutes
Number of portions: 6

Required Material:

- 1.361g of beef stew
- 1 onion, diced
- 4 carrots, diced

- 227 g baby portabella mushrooms, sliced
- 680 ml of beef broth
- 425 g diced tomatoes, canned
- 3 TBSPs of white flour
- 1 tsp of dried basil leaves
- 1 tsp of dried thyme leaves
- 1 tsp of salt
- 1 tsp of pepper
- dried parsley

Procedure step by step:
1. The air fryer is now ready for the meat to be put inside of it so that it may be cooked.
2. After you have placed the carrots in the air fryer, proceed to add the tomatoes, spices, and other herbs (including basil, thyme, salt, and pepper).
3. Replace the lid when you have finished using the disc.
4. High-temperature cooking for one hour and thirty-five minutes while the pot is under pressure.
5. Carefully unscrew the lid, and then quickly let off the pressure.
6. Once the mushrooms have been properly blended with the other ingredients, the soup is ready to be served.

Dietary composition:
Calories: 361, Total Fat: 12 g, Saturated Fat: 5 g, Cholesterol: 117 mg, Sodium: 821 mg, Total Carbohydrates: 15 g, Dietary Fiber: 3 g, Sugars: 6 g, Protein: 48 g

124. Crushed Lentil Soup

Preparing time: 10 minutes
Time needed to cook: 30 minutes
Number of portions: 8

Required Material:
- 2 TBSPs vegetable broth
- 1 onion, finely chopped
- 4 garlic cloves, minced
- 960 ml unsalted vegetable broth

- 480 ml of water
- 480 ml red split lentils
- 1 small pinch saffron
- 1 tsp coriander
- 1 tsp cumin
- ½ tsp freshly ground black pepper
- 1 tsp sea salt
- ½ tsp of red pepper flakes
- 2 bay leaves
- 2 TBSPs fresh lemon juice

Procedure step by step:
1. To sauté the vegetables in the air fryer, start by adding 30 ml of vegetable stock. When the veggies are almost cooked, add the garlic and onions and continue boiling for another four or five minutes.
2. Except for the bay leaves and the lemon juice, toss everything else into the basin. After you have given the meal a good toss, you should cover it and switch off the air fryer.
3. To access the soup selection, just touch the cancel button. Set a timer for 30 minutes and get started. If the pressure has not dropped after 30 minutes, give it another 20.
4. Removing the top and whisking in the bay leaves and lemon juice after the first 5 minutes.
5. Take off the bay leaves before serving.

Dietary composition:
Calories: 250, Total Fat: 1 g, Sodium: 590 mg, Total Carbohydrates: 43 g, Dietary Fiber: 17 g, Sugars: 4 g, Protein: 19 g

125. Asparagus Garlic Ham Soup

Preparing time: 15 minutes
Time needed to cook: 50 minutes
Number of portions: 4

Required Material:
- 680 g asparagus, chopped
- 960 ml chicken stock

- 2 tsp. garlic, minced
- 3 tbsp. olive oil
- 1 onion, diced
- ¾ cup ham, diced
- ½ tsp. thyme

Procedure step by step:

1. Place a little oil in the air fryer, and then set it to Sauté.
2. To cook the onion, sauté it in butter for four minutes.
3. Put the ham and garlic in the microwave for one minute.
4. Make it by letting it cook in stock with thyme. Blend well.
5. Cook for 45 minutes with the lid on while using the Soup setting.
6. Let the air in the pressure cooker out right away, mix the contents, and serve.

Dietary composition:

Calories: 23, Total Fat: 15 g, Saturated Fat: 3 g, Cholesterol: 15 mg, Sodium: 720 mg, Total Carbohydrates: 12 g, Dietary Fiber: 4 g, Sugars: 5 g, Protein: 13 g

126.   Mushroom Chicken Soup

Preparing time: 10 minutes
Time needed to cook: 25 minutes
Number of portions: 4

Required Material:

- 454 g chicken breast, cut into chunks
- 1 tsp. Italian seasoning
- 591 ml chicken stock
- 1 small yellow squash, chopped
- 454 g mushrooms, sliced
- 2 garlic cloves, minced
- 1 onion, sliced
- 1 tsp. black pepper
- 1 tsp. salt

Procedure step by step:

1. Just throw everything in the air fryer and give it a good swirl.

2. Turn the pressure cooker to manual high and cook for 15 minutes.
3. After 10 minutes, relieve the pressure using the quick-release instructions.
4. After the chicken has been removed from the saucepan, the vegetable mixture may be blended until smooth.
5. Using a fork, shred the chicken. 5. Stir the shredded chicken back into the saucepan.
6. Sixth, have fun with it.

Dietary composition:

Calories: 182, Fat: 3g, Saturated Fat: 1g, Cholesterol: 81mg, Sodium: 1022mg, Carbohydrates: 7g, Fiber: 2g, Sugar: 3g, Protein: 31g

127.   Kale Cottage Cheese Soup

Preparing time: 5 minutes
Time needed to cook: 5 minutes
Number of portions: 4

Required Material:

- 1180 ml fresh kale, chopped
- 1 tbsp. olive oil
- 240 g cottage cheese, cut into small chunks
- 710 ml chicken broth
- ½ tsp. black pepper
- ½ tsp. sea salt

Procedure step by step:

1. Toss all of the ingredients, except the cottage cheese, into the air fryer and mix well.
2. Make sure the lid is on tight, then set the pressure cooker to high manual pressure for 5 minutes.
3. Quickly releasing some of the pressure within the container before taking off the top.
4. Mix up some high-quality cottage cheese.
5. Eat when still hot.

Dietary composition:

Calories: 160, Fat: 9g, Carbohydrates: 10g,

Protein: 11g, Fiber: 2g, Sugar: 5g, Sodium: 1070mg

128.   Pearl Barley Soup

Preparing time: 10 minutes
Time needed to cook: 25 minutes
Number of portions: 66

Required Material:
- 120 g all-purpose flour
- 2 onions, chopped
- 2 celery stalks, chopped
- 2 carrots, chopped
- 4 TBSPs olive oil
- 454 g mushroom, sliced
- 790 ml. vegetable stock
- 150 g pearl barley
- 2 tsps dried oregano
- 240 ml purple wine
- Salt and pepper, to taste

Procedure step by step:
1. Choose "Sauté" on the Air fryer's menu and add the oil, garlic, and onions.
2. After 3 minutes of cooking, add the other ingredients to the pan.
3. Select "Soup" from the Air fryer's menu and cook at high pressure for 15 minutes.
4. Turn off the heat source and serve immediately while still hot.

Dietary composition:
Calories: 175, Fat: 6g, Carbohydrates: 24g, Protein: 4g, Fiber: 4g, Sugar: 4g, Sodium: 496m

129.   Currant Pudding

Preparing time: 25 minutes
Number of portions: 6

Required Material:
- 245g red currants, blended
- 240g coconut cream
- 245g black currants, blended
- 3 tbsp. stevia

Procedure step by step:
1. Toss everything into a large bowl and stir until combined.
2. You may bake the ramekins at 170 degrees Celsius for 20 minutes after you pour the batter inside.
3. The most delicious pudding is the cold kind.

Dietary composition:
Calories: 101, Fat: 8g, Carbohydrates: 8g, Fiber: 2g, Sugar: 3g, Protein: 1g

130.   Lemon Blackberries Cake

Preparing time: 35 minutes
Number of portions: 4

Required Material:
- 2 eggs, whisked
- 60ml almond milk
- 150g almond flour
- 140g blackberries; chopped.
- 2 tbsp. ghee; melted
- 4 tbsp. swerve
- 1 tsp. lemon zest, grated
- 1 tsp. lemon juice

- 2.5g. baking powder

Procedure step by step:
1. Simply put all the ingredients in a bowl and whisk them together.
2. Then, bake at 170 degrees Celsius for 25 minutes in a cake pan that can withstand the heat of an air fryer. Cool the cake completely before serving.

Dietary composition:
Calories: 335, Fat: 29g, Carbohydrates: 16g, Fiber: 6g, Protein: 11g

131.   Yogurt Cake

Preparing time: 35 minutes
Number of portions: 12

Required Material:
- 6 eggs, whisked
- 227g Greek yogurt
- 255g coconut flour
- 4 tbsp. stevia
- 1 tsp. vanilla extract
- 1 tsp. baking powder

Procedure step by step:
1. Simply put all the ingredients in a bowl and whisk them together.
2. Put the batter in a cake pan that can go into an air fryer, coated with parchment paper.
3. For 30 minutes in an air fryer, heat to 165 degrees Celsius.

Dietary composition:
Calories: 138 kcal, Total Fat: 4.4 g, Cholesterol: 98 mg, Sodium: 94 mg, Total Carbohydrates: 16.5 g, Fiber: 8.8 g, Sugars: 3.5 g, Protein: 10.6 g

132.   Currant Cookies

Preparing time: 35 minutes
Number of portions: 6

Required Material:
- 75g currants

- 96g swerve
- 224g almond flour
- 112g ghee; melted
- 1 tsp. vanilla extract
- 2 tsp. baking soda

Procedure step by step:
1. Step 1 is Put everything in a bowl and whisk until smooth.
2. To prepare, just spread the mixture on a parchment-lined baking sheet, place the pan in an air fryer set to 175 degrees Celsius, and cook for 30 minutes.
3. Let it cool, then slice it into squares.

Dietary composition:
Calories: 318, Total Fat: 30g, Cholesterol: 31mg, Sodium: 661mg, Total Carbohydrates: 10g, Fiber: 5g, Sugars: 1g, Protein: 8g

133.   Spiced Avocado Pudding

Preparing time: 30 minutes
Number of portions: 6

Required Material:
- 4 small avocados, peeled, pitted, and mashed
- 2 eggs, whisked
- 150g swerve
- 240ml coconut milk
- 1 tsp. cinnamon powder
- ½ tsp. ginger powder

Procedure step by step:
1. Place all the ingredients in a bowl and mix them together well.
2. Fill a pudding mold with the mixture, and bake in an air fryer at 175 degrees Celsius for 25 minutes. Assist amiably

Dietary composition:
Calories: 315, Total Fat: 26g, Cholesterol: 62mg, Sodium: 50mg, Total Carbohydrates: 19g, Fiber: 11g, Sugars: 1g, Protein: 6g

134. Dried Raspberries

Preparing time: 10 minutes
Time needed to cook: 15 hours
Number of portions: 4

Required Material:

- 570g raspberries, wash and dry
- 60ml fresh lemon juice

Procedure step by step:

1. Place some lemon juice and fresh raspberries in a bowl, then combine the two ingredients.
2. Put the raspberries into an oven preheated to 135 degrees Celsius, and let them there for 12 to 15 hours.
3. Maintain In an airtight container seal to avoid oxidation.

Dietary composition:

Calories: 76, Total Fat: 1g, Sodium: 1mg, Total Carbohydrates: 18g, Fiber: 9g., Sugars: 9g, Protein: 2g.

135. Lemon Cookies

Preparing time: 30 minutes
Number of portions: 12

Required Material:

- 60g cashew butter, soft
- 1 egg, whisked
- 180g swerve
- 240ml coconut cream
- Juice of 1 lemon
- 1 tsp. baking powder
- 1 tsp. lemon peel, grated

Procedure step by step:

1. To begin, gather all of the components and mix them together in a bowl.
2. Flatten the balls you just made by spooning them onto a baking sheet covered with parchment paper.
3. Fry the cookie sheet at 175 degrees Celsius for 20 minutes. Cold cookies

should be served.

Dietary composition:

Calories: 148, Total Fat: 13g, Cholesterol: 20mg, Sodium: 103mg, Total Carbohydrates: 9g, Fiber: 2g, Sugars: 1g, Protein: 3g

136. Chocolate Strawberry Cups

Preparing time: 15 minutes
Number of portions: 8

Required Material:

- 16 strawberries; halved
- 360g chocolate chips; melted
- 2 tbsp. coconut oil

Procedure step by step:

1. Strawberries, oil, and melted chocolate chips, tossed gently, then cooked in an air fryer at 170 degrees Celsius for 10 minutes.
2. Pour into cups and refrigerate.

Dietary composition:

Calories: 246; Fat: 19g; Fiber: 3g; Carbs: 22g; Protein: 2g

137. Fruity Oreo Muffins

Preparing time: 15 minutes
Time needed to cook: 10 minutes
Number of portions: 6

Required Material:

- 240ml milk
- 1 pack Oreo biscuits, crushed
- ¾ tsp baking powder
- 1 banana, peeled and chopped
- 1 apple, peeled, cored, and chopped
- 1 tsp cocoa powder
- 1 tsp honey
- 1 tsp fresh lemon juice
- A pinch of ground cinnamon

Procedure step by step:

1. Coat six muffin tins with cooking spray

and set the Air fryer to 160 degrees Celsius.

2. To make the biscuits, mix the milk, cocoa powder, baking soda, and baking powder in a bowl.

3. Then place the batter in the muffin tins and bake for approximately 10 minutes.

4. After four minutes, take the muffins out of the Air fryer and flip them over onto a cooling rack.

5. Meanwhile, in a separate dish, combine the banana, apple, honey, lemon juice, and cinnamon.

6. Hollow out the middle of the muffins and stuff with the fruit mixture.

Dietary composition:
Calories: 232, Fat: 6g, Carbohydrates: 41g, Sugar: 22g, Protein: 4g, Sodium: 226mg

138. Coconut Bars

Preparing time: 5 minutes
Time needed to cook: 40 minutes
Number of portions: 12

Required Material:

- 150g almond flour
- 192g swerve
- 240ml butter, melted
- 120ml coconut cream
- 120g coconut, flaked
- 1 egg yolk
- 85g walnuts, chopped
- ½ tsp extract

Procedure step by step:

1. Combine the flour, half of the swerve, and half of the butter in a bowl; whisk to combine; press the mixture into the bottom of an air fryer-compatible baking pan.

2. Add to the air fryer and cook at 175 degrees C for 15 minutes.

3. Meanwhile, melt the remaining butter in a saucepan over medium heat; whisk in the remaining swerve and the additional

ingredients; simmer for 1-2 minutes; then remove from the heat and let cool.

4. Then, return the pan to the air fryer and cook for another 25 minutes at 175 degrees C, after which you should have a golden crust.

5. Let cool, then slice into bars and serve.

Dietary composition:
Calories 348, Fat 34, Fiber 3, Carbs 9, Sugar 1g, Protein 5

139. Crème Brûlée

Preparing time: 10 minutes
Time needed to cook: 13 minutes
Number of portions: 8

Required Material:

- 10 egg yolks
- 946 ml heavy cream
- 2 TBSPs sugar
- 2 TBSPs vanilla extract

Procedure step by step:

1. Lightly butter 8 (177 ml) ramekins and preheat the Air fryer to 188 degrees C.

2. Add everything in a bowl (except the stevia) and stir until smooth.

3. Then, place the ramekins in the Air fryer after having poured the mixture in.

4. Take away from Air fryer after cooking for about 13 minutes.

5. Once it has cooled somewhat, refrigerate it for three hours before serving.

Dietary composition:
Calories: 442, Fat: 42g, Saturated Fat: 24g, Cholesterol: 419mg, Sodium: 46mg, Carbohydrates: 9g, Sugar: 6g, Protein: 8g

140. Tea Cookies

Preparing time: 15 minutes
Time needed to cook: 25 minutes
Number of portions: 15

Required Material:

- 113.5 g salted butter, softened
- 473 ml almond meal
- 1 organic egg
- 1 tsp ground cinnamon
- 2 tsps sugar
- 1 tsp organic vanilla extract

Procedure step by step:

1. Everything save the stevia should be mixed in a bowl, and then the ramekins should be filled and cooked in an Air fryer.
2. If you are using an air fryer, remove the meal after 13 minutes.
3. Allow at least three hours of refrigeration time before serving.

Dietary composition:

Calories: 173, Fat: 16g, Saturated Fat: 4g, Cholesterol: 24mg, Sodium: 73mg, Carbohydrates: 5g, Fiber: 2g, Sugar: 2g, Protein: 5g

141.   Zucchini Brownies

Preparing time: 5 minutes
Time needed to cook: 35 minutes
Number of portions: 12

Required Material:

- 227 g butter
- 170 g dark chocolate chips
- 355 ml zucchini, shredded
- ¼ tsp baking soda
- 1 egg
- 1 tsp vanilla extract
- 80 ml applesauce, unsweetened
- 1 tsp ground cinnamon
- ½ tsp ground nutmeg

Procedure step by step:

1. Butter eight individual ramekins and prepare an Air fryer to 175 degrees Celsius.

2. Everything save the stevia should be mixed together in a dish.
3. After being packed, the ramekins will be placed in an air fryer for cooking.
4. If you are using an air fryer, remove the food after 13 minutes.
5. Serve chilled; refrigeration for at least three hours is recommended.

Dietary composition:

Calories: 389, Fat: 33g, Saturated Fat: 20g, Cholesterol: 81mg, Sodium: 168mg, Carbohydrates: 20g, Fiber: 3g, Sugar: 14g, Protein: 4g

142.   Lemon Mousse

Preparing time: 15 minutes
Time needed to cook: 10 minutes
Number of portions: 6

Required Material:

- 340 g cream cheese, softened
- ¼ tsp salt
- 1 tsp lemon liquid stevia
- 80 ml fresh lemon juice
- 355 ml heavy cream

Procedure step by step:

1. Prepare an enormous ramekin by buttering it lightly and heating the Air fryer at 175 degrees C.
2. Mix all the ingredients together in a large bowl.
3. After that, you may pop the ramekin into your air fryer.
4. Throw everything into the saucepan and cook on low heat for around 10 minutes.
5. Put it in the fridge for at least three hours to cool, then eat it cold.

Dietary composition:

Calories: 305, Fat: 31g, Carbohydrates: 2.6g, Protein: 5g, Sodium: 279mg

143. Strawberry Cobbler Recipe

Preparing time: 35 Minutes
Number of portions: 6

Required Material:

- 177.44 g sugar
- 900 g strawberries; halved
- 60 g flour
- 1/8 tsp. baking powder
- 119 ml water
- 3 ½ tbsp. EVO oil
- A single tbsp. lemon juice
- Baking soda, just a pinch
- Cooking spray

Procedure step by step:

1. All that is required is a baking dish that can be placed inside of your air fryer, strawberries, sugar half, a dash of flour, a few drops of lemon juice, and a bit of salt. Whisk well

2. In a separate dish, combine the remaining sugar, baking powder, and soda with the flour, and whisk the mixture well.

3. Pour in the olive oil, then thoroughly combine the ingredients using your hands.

4. Combine with a half cup of water, then pour over the fruit and mix. Fry for 25 minutes at 180 degrees Celsius after adding to the oil. Since the cobbler is at its finest when served cold, put it in the refrigerator for a while before slicing it.

Dietary composition:
Calories: 206, Fat: 5.2g, Carbohydrates: 39.8g, Fiber: 3.3g, Protein: 2.3g, Sodium: 20mg

144. Bread Pudding with Cranberry

Number of portions: 4
Time needed to cook: 45 minutes

Ingredients

- 355 ml milk, fat-free
- Eggs: 2-1/2

- 65 g cranberries
- A tsp butter
- 2 TBSPs white sugar
- 40 g raisins golden
- 1/8 tsp cinnamon
- 180 g whipping heavy cream
- 3/4 tsp lemon zest, salt
- 3/4 French baguettes
- 3/8 vanilla beanProcedure step by step:

1. Prepare the air fryer by spraying the baking pan lightly with cooking spray, Baguette slices, dried fruit, and a cranberry-raisin spread.

2. Combine vanilla, cinnamon, salt, lemon, eggs, sugar, cream, all in a blender and mix until smooth. Apply to pieces of baguette. Wait an hour and then use it.

3. Then, use foil to seal the pan.

4. Cook at 165 degrees Celsius for 35 minutes. Cooling ten minutes.

5. Have fun with it.

Dietary composition:
Calories: 484, Fat: 26.3g, Carbohydrates: 52.7g, Sugar: 28.7g, Protein: 10.7g, Sodium: 490mg

145. Oreo Cheesecake

Preparing time: 30 minutes
Number of portions: 8

Required Material:

- 450 g cream cheese
- 1/2 tsp. extract of vanilla
- 4 tbsp. sugar
- 100 g Oreo cookies; crumbled
- 2 eggs; whisked
- 2 tbsp. butter; melted

Procedure step by step:

1. You will need to combine the cookies and butter in a dish, and then press that mixture into the base of a cake pan lined with adequate paper.

2. Then, for 4 minutes at 180 °C, cook the

pan in an air fryer.

3. Spread the sugar, cream cheese, eggs, and vanilla over the crust and stir together until smooth.

4. Fry the cheesecake for 15 minutes at 154 degrees Celsius. The cheesecake should

chill in the fridge for at least two hours before being served.

Dietary composition:

Calories: 432, Fat: 38g, Carbohydrates: 18g, Sugar: 12g, Protein: 8g, Sodium: 381mg

Conclusion

When you fry foods in a regular pan over a gas burner, the heat is not equal across the pan, so your fries will not become crispy and your samosa will not be cooked through. You can make French fries that are just as flawlessly crisp as those you get in restaurants thanks to the deep fryers that are integrated right into your kitchen. Your samosas will have a flawlessly cooked inside and outside. However, this is not the end of the list; it continues on to include things like potato wedges, poultry, and a great deal more. Fryers allow you to produce a variety of foods, from appetizers to main courses, that will delight the taste buds of your loved ones.

The latest models of air fryers are equipped with a variety of capabilities, allowing users to avoid making mistakes during cooking and better appreciate the process overall. The hot water allows you to regulate the temperature according to your preferences, and you may do it manually or electrically, depending on your preference. Reusing the oil and making further use of it is what oil filters do. The stench of frying is mitigated and ultimately removed by the ventilation system. In certain models, you can get automated timers and alarm clocks, which make cooking and frying easier. I am specifically referring to this. In addition, the auto-push and raise function will submerge the frying basket or hold it back so that you may obtain the ideal level of frying.

The question then is: why should you wait? When you are grilling, baking, or frying your food, the last thing you want to do is make a mess in your kitchen, am I right? Invest in an air fryer for yourself. I am grateful for your purchase of this cookbook. I have faith that you will put all of the information you have received to good use.

Conversion Measurement

Measurement:

1 cup = 24 centilitre (cl) or 240 millilitres (ml)
1 TBSP (tbsp) = 15 millilitres (ml)
1 tsp (tsp) = 5 millilitres (ml)
1 fluid ounce (oz) = 30 millilitres (ml)
1 pound (lb) = 454 grams (gm)
16 ounces = 1 pound
1 millilitre = 1/5 tsp
1 millilitre = 0.03 fluid ounce
1 tsp = 5 millilitres
1 TBSP = 15 millilitres
1 fluid ounce = 30 millilitres
1 fluid cup = 236.6 millilitres
1 quart = 946.4 millilitres
1 litre (1000 millilitres) = 34 fluid ounces
1 litre (1000 millilitres) = 4.2 cups
1 litre (1000 millilitres) = 2.1 fluid pints
1 litre (1000 millilitres) = 1.06 fluid quarts
1 litre (1000 millilitres) = 0.26 gallon
1 gallon = 3.8 litres
1 dash = 1/16 tsp
1 pinch = 1/8 tsp

Abbreviations (Standard English)

Cup = c
Fluid cup = fl c
Fluid ounce = fl oz
Fluid quart = fl qt
Foot = ft
Gallon = gal
Inch = in
Ounce = oz
Pint = pt
Pound = lb
Quart = qt
TBSP = t or tbsp
Tsp = t or tsp

Dry Unit, Liquid Unit

1 pint, dry = 1.1636 pints, liquid
1 quart, dry = 1.1636 quarts, liquid
1 gallon, dry = 1.1636 gallons, liquid

CUPS	OUNCES	MILLILITRES	TBSPS
8	64 oz	1895 ml	128
6	48 oz	1420 ml	96
5	40 oz	1180 ml	80
4	32 oz	960 ml	64
2	16 oz	480 ml	32
1	8 oz	240 ml	16
3/4	6 oz	177 ml	12
2/3	5 oz	158 ml	11
½	4 oz	118 ml	8
3/8	3 oz	90 ml	6
1/3	2.5 oz	79 ml	5.5
1/4	2 oz	59 ml	4
1/8	1 oz	30 ml	3
1/16	½ oz	15 ml	1

Temperature:

Conversion formulae

$C = (F - 32) \times 5/9$

$F = (C \times 9/5) + 32$

FAHRENHEIT	CELSIUS
100 °F	37 °C
150 °F	65 °C
200 °F	93 °C
250 °F	121 °C
300 °F	150 °C
325 °F	160 °C
350 °F	180 °C
375 °F	190 °C
400 °F	200 °C
425 °F	220 °C
450 °F	230 °C
500 °F	260 °C
525 °F	274 °C
550 °F	288 °C

Weight:

1 ounce = 28.35 grams
1 pound = 453.59 grams
1 gram = 0.035 ounce
100 grams = 3.5 ounces
1000 grams = 2.2 pounds
1 kilogram = 35 ounces
1 kilogram = 2.2 pounds

IMPERIAL	METRIC
½ oz	15 g
1 oz	29 g
2 oz	57 g
3 oz	85 g
4 oz	113 g
5 oz	141 g
6 oz	170 g
8 oz	227 g
10 oz	283 g
12 oz	340 g
13 oz	369 g
14 oz	397 g
15 oz	425 g
1 lb	453 g

Printed in Great Britain
by Amazon